Of Principals and Projects

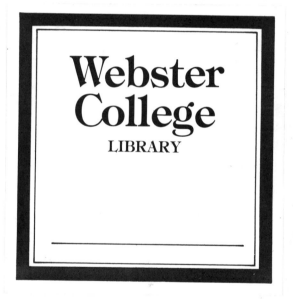

Webster
College
LIBRARY

Of PRINCIPALS *and* PROJECTS

by Spencer H. Wyant

with Diane L. Reinhard *and* Richard I. Arends

Developed by Teachers Corps

Published — Reston, Virginia, 1980 — by

 ASSOCIATION OF TEACHER EDUCATORS

ASSOCIATION OF TEACHER EDUCATORS
Suite ATE, 1900 Association Drive
Reston, Virginia 22091

Library of Congress Catalog Card Number 80-69486

This material was produced pursuant to Contract Number
300-77-0156 between the Center for Urban Education at the
University of Nebraska at Omaha and the Teacher Corps,
United States Office of Education, Department of Health,
Education and Welfare. Contractors undertaking projects
under such government sponsorship are encouraged to freely
express their professional judgment in the conduct of such
projects. Points of view or opinion stated here, therefore, do
not represent official positions or policy of the United States
Office of Education.

Developmental Training Activities Contract
Director: Floyd T. Waterman
Editing and text design by Joan M. Krager
Cover design by Jack Brodie

Table of Contents

v

Foreword

Person in the middle, educational leader, community relations expert, disciplinarian, financial manager—all these terms and more are used to describe the school principal. As societal demands on the schools have grown, the responsibilities of the principal have grown in a geometric progression. At least one state is now experimenting with co-principals, one for administration and one for instruction.

The Association of Teacher Educators, recognizing the need for involvement of principals in teacher education, recently expanded its definition of public school representatives to include principals and other administrators. The increasing involvement and contributions by principals in the deliberations of the Delegate Assembly have proven the wisdom of that decision. However, as is pointed out in this publication, even with the increasing expectations being made of the principal, inservice education for administrators lags far behind what is available for teachers.

Of Principals and Projects looks closely at this and includes some suggestions for improvement. At one point the authors quote from a source regarding proposal writing: ". . . neat, clean, easy to read . . . use English not bureaucratese . . . make it brief . . . be positive." Readers will find that the authors have taken this advice to heart.

The Association of Teacher Educators is pleased to cooperate in bringing this publication to the educational community, particularly the principals, whose assistance and support are so crucial in the task of improving teacher education at all levels.

Robert J. Stevenson
Executive Director
Association of Teacher Educators

Preface

Public schools in America are caught in a squeeze between rising expectations and declining resources. Schools are expected to solve an increasing array of social problems, but enrollment, tax bases, and public support for education are in many cases dwindling.

The person who often feels the crunch most is the man or woman who sits in the principal's chair. The superintendent demands that the principal carry out directives from the central office, parents bring their complaints about the school to the principal's door, and a host of federal agencies inundate the principal with regulations to be followed and reports to be submitted. And nearly every professional journal contains an article calling on the principal to be the "instructional leader" of the school.

Yet principals themselves often feel trapped, caught between what they see as increasing restrictions on their authority imposed by collective bargaining agreements and decreasing support from central office superiors and school boards. Maintaining the routine operation of the school, coping with the daily crises of major or minor proportions, and keeping up with the never-ending "purple flood" of paperwork often leave little time or energy for being the school's educational leader.

Over the past two decades, many special projects funded by federal agencies or other sources external to the school have been tried, and the principal has been expected to provide leadership in implementing them. Yet many principals feel ill prepared to lead the process of change and innovation. A national study by Becker and others (1971) concluded that, while most principals felt they could oversee the routine operation of their building, relatively few had "any degree of confidence in their ability to assume a leadership role in instructional improvement." There is little in the principal's background as a teacher, or in her or his preservice training, that gives adequate preparation for managing externally funded projects.

That lack of preparation is distressing in view of ample evidence that the principal's role is critical to the success or failure of special projects. The principal's support cannot by itself guarantee success to a project, but the literature records case after case in which a change effort failed because of lack of support, unskillful leadership, or active opposition from the principal.

As members of the staff of an externally funded project—the Teacher Corps Youth Advocacy project sponsored by the University of Oregon, the Eugene School District, and Lane County Juvenile Department—and as members of a university that trains administrators, we have an intense interest in how principals affect projects in their schools. We are especially concerned about the kinds of inservice training that can help principals be project leaders. We can be more effective if we know what principals' inservice needs are, and how we can design and deliver training that meets those needs.

We think that others share our concern. Teacher Corps is one of several federal agencies that spend millions of dollars each year on special projects. We believe it is helpful to those agencies to know how to better prepare principals to lead those projects and spend their money wisely. Surely staff development specialists and others who provide inservice education for administrators can benefit from knowledge of the behaviors of principals that most directly influence the course of a project and how to help principals develop leadership skills and facilitating behaviors. Theorists and others who observe schools and try to understand them would probably welcome empirical findings about the effects of the principal's behavior. Finally, we believe that principals themselves can benefit from experienced-based suggestions that help them exert more effective instructional leadership in their schools.

The impetus for this book, then, comes from our desire to learn and communicate to others more effective ways of providing inservice training that helps principals with the crucial tasks of their job. The study upon which this book is based (Reinhard et al., 1979) was conducted under a grant from Teacher Crops to the Cycle XII Teacher Corps project at the University of Oregon, and the writing of the book was supported through a contract with the Center for Urban Education at the University of Nebraska at Omaha. Our special thanks goes to them.

A friend of ours, an historian in Boulder, Colorado, complains that all books in education are written by "so-and-so, him-and-her, and a cast of thousands." Be that as it may, it is true that this book would not have been possible without the contributions, assistance, and cooperation of several dozens of people. We would like to thank all of them personally and publicly. We are prevented from thanking the 79 principals and teachers we interviewed in 14 schools by our promises of confidentiality. We greatly appreciate their willingness to take time from their busy schedules to talk with us and share their insights on the role of principal.

Others deserve special mention. Bill Kutz conducted the initial review of the literature that appears in Chapter 1. Katherine Lovell did a superb job of editing the case studies, creating order and coherence from the diverse reports of the field researchers. Martha Burns ably served as field site coordinator and made sure that everybody made it to the plane on time. Dick Arends, Janet Bullock, Terry Bullock, Martha Burns, Rick Grimes, Ray Hull, Louisa Kozey, Kathy Lovel, Diane Reinhard, and Carol Sivage conducted the field research on which the study was based. Dick Arends and Diane Reinhard were principal investigators for that study. We relied heavily on the able typing assistance of Zola Ehlers, Jeannine Ferguson, Judy Jones, Norma Jones, and Sissel Lemke.

We are indebted to Michael Bishow for her candid criticisms of initial drafts of the manuscript, and her insightful comments and helpful suggestions, and to Joan Krager for her careful editorial assistance.

Finally, we wish to thank Beryl Nelson, Haroldie Spriggs, James Steffensen, and Floyd Waterman for their efforts in helping the study and book see the light of day.

Eugene, Oregon
August 1980   Spencer H. Wyant

Of Principals and Projects

CHAPTER *1*

Spotlight on the Principal

During the past two decades, the federal government and many private and public agencies have sponsored projects aimed at improving public schools. Their common assumption has been that investing resources at the local level to promote important social goals will encourage innovation in schools and improvement of education.

After twenty years, educators are beginning to get some idea of what works and what doesn't. Two conclusions from the accumulated evidence are inescapable: most projects simply haven't worked[1] and the role of the principal has been critical in those few that have succeeded.

We obviously do not believe that the situation is hopeless, even though the evidence is discouraging. Like Miles (1964) we believe that success has as much to do with smart, effective management as does the project itself. Our hopes are twofold: to isolate some critical factors and behaviors of the principal that lead to success and to provide insights into how the principal can increase a project's chances for success.

This first chapter introduces our study of the helpful and unhelpful behaviors of principals in fourteen Oregon schools

[1]For example, Goodland and his associates (1970: 97) concluded that despite a good deal of rhetoric and activity, "changes widely recommended for the schools over the past fifteen years were blunted on the school and classroom door." Silberman (1970: 160), after surveying a variety of innovations and reforms, concluded that most of them turned out to be "more gimmickry and packaging than substantive change." Other investigators have come to similarly gloomy conclusions.

3

with externally funded change projects. We review some of the more important recent studies of change projects in schools,[2] especially those that illuminate what others have found about the principal's role in managing those projects. We also describe the methods we used to gather and analyze the information upon which we base our conclusions and recommendations.

First we review several studies of educational change and externally funded projects which help identify the main issues and central questions of this investigation. We then turn to writings that describe the contemporary role of the principal, especially as it affects the management of projects.

Externally Funded Projects for Educational Change
REVIEW OF CURRICULUM CHANGE

Fullan and Pomfret (1977) reviewed research on curriculum implementation for the National Institute of Education. From a search of ERIC files and dissertation abstracts, they identified 27 studies conducted since 1970 about issues of implementation of new school practices. Most concerned change in curriculum, but the authors also included studies of organizational changes such as differentiated staffing and open education. The most significant finding of the Fullan and Pomfret review is that introducing and implementing change in schools is far more difficult and complex than most people believe. Most efforts are unsuccessful and issues of implementation (actual use) have not been considered as thoroughly as those associated with adoption (intended use).

Fullan and Pomfret recommend that implementers should conceive implementation as a negotiation process characterized by conflict over goals, means, and resources, and that they should provide structures and support for users to define their own needs and to develop or choose their own solutions.

[2]The literature on educational change is immense. We have not tried to provide a thorough review of it because others have already done that: Hall and Alford, 1976; Emerick, Peterson, and Agarwala-Rogers, 1977; Paul, 1977; among others. Useful bibliographies are Maguire, Temkin, and Cummings, 1971; and Runkel and Burr, 1977.

Even though Fullan and Pomfret do not go into specifics about the role of the principal in the change process, they do, in numerous instances, refer to the importance of administrative *support* if change efforts are to be successful.

THE RAND STUDIES

Under sponsorship of the U.S. Office of Education, the Rand Corporation in 1975 concluded a multi-year investigation of federally funded change programs. Surveys of 293 projects and 29 case studies were conducted in change programs funded by various federal agencies, including Title III—Innovative Projects, Title VII, Bilingual Projects, Vocational Education Act's Exemplary Programs, and Right-to-Read Programs.

As with the studies reviewed by Fullan and Pomfret, the Rand Studies by Berman and McLaughlin (1975) document the complexity and lack of success of many educational change projects. Among other conclusions, they found four conditions necessary for successful implementation:

- a receptive institutional setting characterized by a problem-solving attitude rather than opportunism for available funds;
- involvement of local participants in planning and the promotion of mutual adaptation;
- provision of staff training tailored to the local setting and conducted by local personnel;
- provision for "repackaging" of existing products or providing new project materials, e.g., combining materials for teaching reading that come from a number of publishing houses.

The Rand researchers (Berman and McLaughlin, 1975; Mann, 1976) also reported that the projects which accomplished the least were redirected or subverted by the principal. Projects which were unsuccessful directly challenged the principal's leadership and tried to move teachers away from practices sanctioned by the principal. Endorsement and active

5

support by principals were almost always necessary for success.

PROJECT ON SOCIAL ARCHITECTURE IN EDUCATION

More insight about the principal's role is provided by a recent study (Miles 1978b) on the creation of six new schools. The Project on Social Architecture in Education included a strategy of planning and implementing new schools to promote educational improvement. One goal of the study was to describe empirical stages in the social-architectural process, linkages between the stages in the social-architectural process, and methods of facilitating effective school design and start-up.

In one school deemed successful by the "project architects" the principal's social support of parents and teachers was *crucial*. Another school facing difficult implementation problems was not as fortunate: internal coordination and problem-solving were poor, and the *principal provided little support*. He later resigned. Where the principal was not committed to the innovation, few goals were achieved. Among other conclusions, Miles found that the principal's personal predictability and consistency were more important to project success than was the leadership style used.

STUDIES ON ORGANIZATIONAL CHANGE

Researchers in the Program on Strategies for Organizational Change (SOC) at the University of Oregon's Center for Educational Policy and Management (CEPM) have been studying the processes of school improvement since 1967. In several publications they refer to the importance of the principal in facilitating or restraining change efforts in schools. In one early project (Runkel, Wyant, Bell, and Runkel, 1980) they found that innovative efforts stayed more firmly planted in schools in which the principal remained throughout the effort. A follow-up study on the durability of change in one of SOC's early projects (Simons, 1974) found that favorable effects of training decreased substantially after a new principal took over

6

the school. In a later project aimed at assisting several elementary schools convert from traditional self-contained classrooms to multi-unit, team-teaching arrangements, willingness of the principal to change his own behavior to support the new structure was critical to success (see Schmuck, Murray, Smith, Schwartz, and M. Runkel, 1975; Starling, 1973; Smith, 1972).

In another project, the SOC researchers trained a cadre of teachers, principals, and others in a school district to provide training in organizational development to schools and other subsystems. (The project is described in Arends and Phelps, 1973; Schmuck, Runkel, Arends, and Arends, 1977). Bell (1977) studied the efforts of the cadre to see if organizational training provided by them was effective in improving such organizational processes as communication, problem-solving, decision-making, and the like. He found that there was some relationship between training and effective organizational processes but—more importantly for this study—organizational process were most effective in schools in which the principals had received large amounts of training.

In a more recent project, the SOC researchers studied ways of transmitting knowledge from one school to another and processes that would enhance urban schools' capacity for problem-solving. Several intitial results speak to the role of the principal in change processes. For example, the CEPM researchers (Runkel, Schmuck, Arends, and Francisco, 1979: 108, 110, 111) note the importance of:

1. Willingness of the administrator to support changes in the roles of others by making reciprocal changes in his or her own role. (Change is much more difficult when the administrator says, "You go ahead and change, but don't ask me to do so.")
2. Degree of support given by administrators to a change project or to maintaining the present pattern of stability. (Giving support means giving some sort of resource: services, materials, money, information, status, or affection.)
3. Individuals' confidence that key administrators will continue in his or her position until at least a year after the target of the problem solving has been reached. (If too many members of a school believe

7

the principal is likely to depart while the problem solving is under way or before it has become institutionalized, they will worry that the next principal may not support the work.)

Studies of Educational Dissemination and Change.—Throughout the 1970s, the federal government has promoted projects aimed at improving the flow of knowledge and exemplary school practices from one setting to another. These activities have produced a number of significant investigations that, like others we have discussed, illuminate the processes of change in public schools and the role the principal plays in that process.

The first of these projects, known as the Pilot State Dissemination Project, was sponsored by the U.S. Office of Education in 1970. In three states, educational field agents (similar to agricultural extension agents) were hired to disseminate information to local school personnel to improve school practices. The researchers (Sieber et. al., 1972) found that agents used local power structures, particularly principals and superintendents, to gain entry to teachers and other school site personnel. Administrative support was an important element in any success they experienced.

In 1974, the U.S. Office of Education established the National Diffusion Network (NDN). This project employed in various states facilitators or change agents whose mission was to get local educational agencies to adopt innovative programs "validated" by research and evaluation.

Emrick and his colleagues (1977) reported that successful projects were those that had early involvement of administrative and instructional decision-makers within the schools. As with the Pilot State Dissemination study, agents had to work through local power structures and administrators to get to teachers and other site personnel. Change was unlikely unless both the superintendent and principal concurred and gave their permission.

In summary, a decade of research has given us some important information about the process of change in schools; all findings seem to indicate that, without the principal's active

8

support and endorsement, almost any effort by outsiders will fail.

Focus on the Principal

Just as a body of research evidence emphasizes the importance of the principal's role in school improvement efforts, theorists on school administration have also been concerned about the principal's role in educational improvement. The volume of literature on school administration and the principal's role is large indeed. (For example, Firth [1976] found nearly 620 works on leadership in administration, curriculum, instruction, and supervision during the eight-year period 1968–75). Not surprisingly, most of the literature emphasizes the importance of the principal's role. Miles (1964) pointed out that without the support of key administrators little chance of educational improvement exists. More recently, Lipham (1977: 118) wrote:

> The administrator is positioned at the critical confluence of the intraorganizational and extraorganizational forces which either foster or impede educational change and improvement. Although much has been written to date regarding the routine managerial aspects of the administrator's role, less has been said about the role of the administrator in fostering educational improvement; and still less is known about the unique linking functions of the local school administrator.

Sarason (1971: 111) states, "We begin with the principal because any kind of system change puts him in the role of *implementing* change in his school." Identifying the principal as a key change agent is no longer a novel idea; indeed, it has become a piece of accepted wisdom in the literature on change.

Being the focal point of school change is like facing a firing squad, each soldier armed with a different kind of weapon. No uniform expectation exists for the principal's role, and thus she or he is vulnerable to a myriad of internal and external demands. At some point, those demands have their price.

The principal in many ways is a person overworked, facing major role conflict, and unable to manage the demands of the

9

job itself, much less lead a faculty toward major innovation and change. For example, the March 13, 1978, issue of *Newsweek* reported a national study of 1,600 principals, conducted by the National Association of Secondary School Principals (McCleary and Thomson, 1979), which described the changing and sometimes contradictory expectations of the principal's role in a society where expectations for "good" schools are shifting rapidly. The principal's door is increasingly the place where competing demands are confronted:

> At Denver's Adams High School, William Van Buskirk smoothed crisis after crisis—walkouts by political radicals, riots by angry Chicanos, even gun play in the halls—while maintaining an admirable educational program. His efforts won him the nomination by local educators in 1975 as one of Colorado's outstanding principals. But Van Buskirk paid a heavy price. He worked seven days and five nights a week until he grew exhausted, physically and emotionally; he also ended up in divorce court. After eight years on the job, Van Buskirk quit to open a less-taxing consulting firm. "You're supposed to be a miracle worker" he says of his old position, "but nobody offers to help the principal on his job. I felt alone." (*Newsweek*, March 13, 1978)

Van Buskirk's experience illustrates our belief that the principalship is a job in which there are too many expectations and not enough support for trying to meet them.

One consequence of these demands and conditions for the administrator is too often stress, uncertainty, and feelings of impotence and ineffectiveness. A recent survey by Gmelch (1977: 19) shows that administrators feel especially stressed by complying with a myriad of rules, meetings, paperwork, gaining public approval and financial support for school programs, resolving school-parent conflicts, evaluating staff, and even the interruptions of telephone calls. As much as three-fourths of an administrator's day may be unplanned, given over to administration by crisis. At times it seems as though the principal's job is divided between crises and administrivia,[3] with no time left for instructional leadership.

The dilemma of the principal is well illustrated in Harry Wolcott's study (1973), *The Man in the Principal's Office*. Wol-

10

cott "shadowed" an elementary school principal for an entire school year to find where his time, energies, and attention were spent. As noted in the introduction:

> it is clear that the principal's role is that of mediator rather than innovator or commander. Much of his time and energy is devoted to conflict resolution or the prevention of conflicts latent in the system of interrelationships. It is also clear that with this emphasis on the mediator's role, it is impossible for the principal to attend in any depth to the educational process itself. (pp. viii–ix)

The split within the literature reflects the contemporary principals' position between a rock and a hard place. When one reads this literature or listens to the discussions, two facts stand out. One, there is an interesting set of mixed messages about how much power and influence the principal actually has. Two, there is a striking lack of information about what principals actually do or do not do that leads to the success or failure of change projects.

On the one hand, messages from those who study change in schools describe the principalship as the key position around which all improvement efforts pivot. Outside change agents are informed that without the endorsement and active support of principals or without a principal's active involvement, efforts at school improvement are doomed to failure. Principals themsleves are told they are the "gatekeepers of change" and encouraged to exercise their leadership.

On the other hand, practitioners themselves often describe the principal as a powerless functionary caught in the middle of a myraid of internal and external demands and unable to influence the direction of events in any siginificant way.

A recent study (Blood, 1978) by the New Mexico state legislature and the University of New Mexico found that the principalship is a job with too many expectations and not

---

[3]We first heard this delightfully descriptive word from some teachers in a Colorado school district, who usually used it in the same breath with "snoopervision" and who ordinarily referred to the district office as "Fort Fumble." It is one of the more printable descriptions of teachers' perceptions of the kinds of tasks that divert the principal's attention from teachers, students, and learning.

11

enough time or authority to accomplish them. Looking at both job descriptions and the way the job is actually carried out, the study concluded:

> Irrespective of the rhetoric of intent, the role of the principal is formally conceived as primarily administrative and managerial. The expectations for casting the principal as the "educational leader" are simply not borne out. Almost 86 per cent of the duties are administrative and managerial. (*Education USA*, May 21, 1979: 293)

Sarson (1971) titles one section of his book, *The Culture of the School and the Problem of Change*, as "The Principal as Scapegoat." He notes that

> When most people think about a school principal they almost always think in terms of what a principal can do, and attribute to him a good deal of power and freedom to act in his school. They rarely will think in terms of what he cannot do or the numerous restrictions, formal and informal, that limit his freedom of action. This tendency to think in terms of, and to over-evaluate, the power of the principal is . . . mistaken. (p. 119)

The contemporary principal is increasingly called on to perform many roles, which can be categorized as the principal as instructional leader (Gaye, 1979); principal as business administrator; principal as manager (Lipham, 1977); and principal as linker, facilitator, human relations/resource specialist (Schmuck and Nelson, 1970), hereafter referred to as organizational facilitator.

The first role deals with the routine management of the school, which involves working through individuals and groups to accomplish organizational goals. The major managerial functions are planning, organizing, motivating, and controlling. Planning involves setting goals and objectives for the organization. Organizing involves the integration of resources (e.g., people, materials). Motivating is influencing others to reach the goals. Controlling must account for the discrepancy between plans and results with an emphasis on making the appropriate adjustments (Hersey and Blanchard, 1977). Increasingly, the principal must be a business manager, acquiring and allocating human and other resources needed to maintain the school's program and physical plant.

Most theorists (and job descriptions) call on the principal to be the school's instructional leader. Gaye (1979) points out that principals must take a leadership role in instruction because: (1) the school program is becoming increasingly complex and one person must orchestrate this complexity; (2) reduced resources for curriculum leadership require that the principal play a more assertive role; (3) curriculum innovations demand that principals be aware and capable of using new methods to promote teacher effectiveness; and (4) the pluralism of pupil needs obligates the principal to manage a total, consistent, and congruent program for all.

Not everyone agrees that the principal should play an instructional leadership role. Some school faculty believe that this role is their prerogative. Others believe one person can't possibly be aware of all the latest instructional programs and their advantages and disadvantages. Sarason, in his conversation with teachers, asked why a principal was needed. He found that:

> a variety of answers were given and they tended to have one thing in common: there are "practical" matters of an everyday sort (that do or could occur) which could bring operations of a school to a halt if the principal were not present. Who would keep the attendance data? Order supplies? Handle behavior problems and sick children? Supervise fire drills? Talk to parents when they phoned or visited? One could go on listing housekeeping matters which were considered to require the presence of a principal. What is most interesting to me is that teachers rarely, if ever, responded in terms of . . . the principal's educational or leadership role, his evaluation function, his role as a representative of the teachers to other administrative bodies . . . .
> (1971: 114)

Despite Sarason's statement, we continue to believe that instructional leadership is an important part of the principal's role, though it is one for which principals often have inadequate preparation or support.

To carry out this instructional leadership role will require the use of another leadership role or style. The literature has

13

various terms: convener, coordinator, human relations expert, or facilitator. We are using organizational facilitator. The term "facilitator of external change" differentiates the role from one of merely linking needs and resources or convening of faculty meetings. Schmuck and Nelson (1970) are concerned that organizational change occur through more attention to surfacing conflict, greater participation in decision-making, and greater school-wide problem-solving. Bockman (1972) echoes a similar plan. She emphasizes the processes of active and creative leadership over simply administering predetermined policies. Tomplins and Trump (1969) suggest that the principal give more attention to his or her communication skills, informal and horizontal organizational forms, and delegation of much more decision-making. The positions appear consistent with the recent findings of the federal change project studies.

In short, the expectations and demands placed on the principal are diverse and often conflicting. It should come as no surprise that many principals and staffs we interviewed expressed confusion and conflict about the proper role for the principal in leading externally funded change projects. Should the principal be a business manager? An instructional leader? Organizational facilitator? Traditional manager? All of these? We found that principals were called on to play all those roles. Whether they were successful in doing so depended on how well the role they played matched the demands of the task and the expectations of teachers.

In summary, several strands of the recent professional literature point to the importance of the principal's role in initiating and sustaining change in schools. Reports such as the Rand study on federally funded efforts, studies of curriculum change, descriptions of organizational change, studies of educational dissemination and change, and statements by theorists underline the importance of the principal's influence. However, none of these works is very specific in identifying the particular behaviors that make a difference or in identifying the inservice needs of building administrators. A few recent surveys have identified needs for inservice education as

14

described by building administrators, but the needs they identify are fairly vague and incomplete.

If anything, a review of the literature has confirmed our perception that there is a desperate need to identify principal behaviors that are helpful and unhelpful in initiating and sustaining externally funded change projects. Identifying those behaviors can serve as the basis for specifying objectives and procedures for improving principals' capacities to perform this aspect of their role.

Method

Knowing how to collect information requires that you have a sense of what you want to know about the problem and how much you already know. Our first task, then, was to think through these issues.

Our charge from the funding agency was to study "the inservice needs of building administrators." That covers a wide range of possible needs and of strategies for meeting them, so we had to narrow our focus. We decided to restrict our study to those behaviors that are valuable for principals in administering school-based innovations funded by outside sources. The special nature of these projects—even though they vary widely in funding sources, scope of the proposed change, and other dimensions—is that they call into play a wide range of behaviors, ones which are different from those needed in the ordinary, day-to-day management of the school. These projects require the principal in some sense to be a "leader" as well as "manager"; they highlight the role of the principal as the pivotal one in the school, the one upon which various publics, constituencies, authorities, and interest groups bring pressure to bear. (The principal must be the liaison between the regular and project staff, between the school and the district office, between the school and its community, and so on.) They place special demands on all concerned, thus increasing existing pressures or releasing existing resources, so that a study of special projects provides a "critical incident" that highlights many features of the system that

15

would not otherwise be observed. They are the feature of schools most relevant to the concerns of the funding agency—how to improve the chances for successful implementation of Teacher Corps and other externally funded projects. Finally, managing projects such as these are one aspect of the principal's job which is too often neglected in the principal's preservice or inservice training; it is unlikely that one would find in course descriptions of universities that train administrators a title such as "How to Successfully Manage a Special Project in Your School."

With this narrowed focus in hand, we then addressed the question of how much was already known about the problem. We were faced with the choice between two strategies. The first strategy would work if the behaviors needed by principals to support special projects had already been defined and if findings reported in the literature were trustworthy guides. To conduct the study using that strategy, we would first have identified behaviors described as important in the literature, constructed a survey based on them, administered a mail survey or questionnaire to a large sample of administrators, tallied the results, and drawn our conclusions about what kinds of behaviors were helpful and unhelpful.

Our review of the literature, our own experience in conducting inservice for administrators, and our contacts with the funding agencies as to their preferences convinced us that this was an unwise strategy. The problem was simply not well enough defined to permit a rigorous testing of already held ideas.

A second strategy seemed more promising. In this strategy, one assumes that the problem is not well defined and that one must do some unstructured "poking around" to find out what is going on. Further, we wanted to be sure that the problems we would be asking questions about were defined by the practitioners themselves. Also, we needed a strategy that would give us a "broad band" of information about the principal and the change project, one that would reveal the context, interactions, and settings that affected the projects. Change projects in schools are affected by a wide variety of factors; we did not want to risk too narrow a focus which would give us answers that ignored or eliminated these factors. Finally, we wanted to get a variety of perspectives, asking not only the principal what his or her inservice needs were, or how the principal behaved in relation to the project, but also asking other persons affected how they viewed helpful and unhelpful behaviors of the principal. (One of the case studies confirmed the wisdom of that approach, because the perceptions of the principal and of others involved in the project were widely divergent.)

We identified our major purposes as understanding better the role of the principal in supporting school-based innovations, discovering which skills and attitudes were needed, and exploring how they could be taught in inservice actitivities. We were especially interested in new ideas for the delivery of inservice training. We wanted to find answers to several questions: How does a principal respond in a helpful way to an externally funded project in his or her school? How does a principal respond in an unhelpful way? What are current conceptions of the needs, problems, and opportunities regarding inservice for principals?

All in all, the nature of the problem and the information that already existed clearly seemed to point toward an in-depth study of a few projects rather than a superficial or narrow study of many projects. In short, we were looking at some variations of a case study approach rather than a survey questionnaire approach.

The decision to use a case study or field study approach rather than a survey meant that we spent a considerable amount of time on concerns of method. We had to select appropriate sites, train people to conduct site visits and interviews, write up the cases, and analyze the information. We think it was worth it. The cases provided rich descriptions of the principals in their natural environments full of stress, problems, and rays of hope.

Our method is hard to label, and it does not fit neatly into any of the various categories suggested by persons who think about this kind of study. It is neither enthography, nor comprehensive case study, nor portrayal, nor even "educational story-telling." We came to call each description of a site a "mini case study." Before designing the specific procedures used by field researchers, we reviewed the literature on ethnography, naturalistic inquiry, and case study to develop conceptual frameworks and strategies and methods.[4]

In outline, the procedures we finally settled upon were these:

1. Identify 10 to 15 schools in Oregon to serve as sites for case studies.
2. Train people to go to the site for several days to review pertinent documents, to observe, and to interview administrators, teachers, and project staff.
3. Compare data from case studies to determine patterns and to identify the most common inservice needs.
4. Write a report describing helpful and unhelpful behaviors of principals, administrators' needs for inservice, and what it means to be a principal with a special project in one's school.

In designing specific procedures for the study, we relied on a variety of sources. Particularly helpful were the field work guidelines proposed by Stake (1977), the methodology used in the recently completed National Science Foundation Science Multiple Case Study (Stake and Easley, 1978), the issues raised by Denny in "Story Telling and Educational Understanding" (1979), and the propositions of Wolf and Tymitz (1978) for field work in museums. We also became aware of a variety of problems encountered in field work as described in Guba's monograph, *Toward a Methodology of Naturalistic Inquiry in Educational Evaluation* (1978), and as identified by Miles (1978a).

---

[4]In particular, we found the ideas Stake (1976) describes in "The Logic of the Case Study" particularly helpful.

The 14 mini cases were completed by ten researchers, some of whom had never engaged in this type of field work. The field researchers all had fairly substantial backgrounds in education. All were members of the College of Education of the University of Oregon; of the ten persons who completed case studies, two had both teaching and administrative duties, three had teaching and research duties, and three were graduate students; also included were the project's administrative assistant and one spouse who acompanied her husband on the site visit. In a series of training meetings, the researchers learned some of the basic issues of methodology and discussed literature dealing with methodology, different concepts of the role of principal, and the issues inherent in each. We decided upon interview protocols. We discussed the first two site visits in some detail to refine procedures for the remaining visits. Finally, we adopted a format for case descriptions. Each investigator had a master packet of instructions, interview protocols, outlines, consent forms, and travel worksheet. The interview form used with principals is presented in the Appendix.

Field researchers followed these steps in completing a mini case study.

1. Select site from list of potential schools.
2. Contact principal and determine interest in participation.
3. Set up time for visit.
4. Identify people to be interviewed. Identify on-site assistant for setting up interviews.
5. Request informational material about community, school, and project. Review this material in advance.
6. Determine whether district-level approval is needed for this study. Obtain approval if necessary.
7. Follow up original contact with letter that summarizes agreements reached.
8. Review case study methodology, interview protocols, issues.

19

9. Travel to site, check in with principal, reaffirm interview schedule.
10. Conduct interviews, review documents, obtain signed consent forms, including protection of human subjects forms.
11. Review raw data; collect additional data as necessary.
12. Send thank-you letter to site.
13. Review all data; write case study in recommended format.

Field researchers spent an average of two days at each site. They conducted 79 interviews of 21 principals or administrative team members, 16 project staff workers, and 42 teachers. Each case write-up took an additional two or three days.

Principals were asked to provide information about the project and their involvement in it, specifically:

1. *Initiation.*—How did the principal become aware of the project; what were his or her initial reactions, feelings, and opinions about it; and what was the principal's role in initiating the project?
2. *Early implementation.*—How were needs for the project identified and how was the staff involved in identifying the needs, and how much responsibility for meeting the needs was taken by the principal or by the staff?
3. *Later implementation.*—How did the principal's involvement change as the project matured, how was any resistance dealt with, how was the project assimilated into the school, what was the principal's role regarding staff members who were carrying out the project, and what was especially important about the principal's role in relation to the success of the project?
4. *Summarizing involvement.*—What were the key benefits of the project, what were the most important helpful and unhelpful things that the principal did,

20

and were there changes in the principal's perception of the project and the staff?

5. *Inservice needs assessment.*—What inservice activities should have been part of the project to help the principal, what past experience with inservice had the principal had, and what were the strengths and weaknesses of prior inservice experiences in content and format?

6. *The principal.*—Information about the principal himself or herself, including family situation, experience, reasons for becoming an administrator, and other pertinent information.

Teachers and project staff were asked similar questions, the difference being that they were asked about their perceptions of the principal's awareness of the project, support for it, and behaviors in relation to it. They were also asked to describe the leadership style of the principal.

Selecting sites at which to conduct the field studies involved creating criteria that would provide appropriate cases for study, and then searching to find those sites. We identified a number of criteria important in site selection. The external project had to be of sufficient magnitude and serve a specified target population (low-income or otherwise educationally disadvantaged students). The project had to have been functioning in the school for at least a year. The principal had to be willing to participate in our study. The principal or administrative team had to be involved in the project. The principal had to have been at the school for at least a year. We were also concerned with a few other parameters. Sites had to be distributed throughout the state and projects had to represent a variety of grades (from K to 12), types (reading skills, magnet arts, community involvement), and settings (urban, suburban, rural).

We generated a list of potential sites by asking for suggestions from State Department of Education personnel and university personnel working with principals, as well as by examining a list of administrators who had adopted or adapted validated programs and a list of innovative schools. More than 60 schools were on our initial list. First choosing on a random basis and then adjusting the sample to reflect representation of all categories, we came up with 24 schools. Then we assigned field researchers and sought the necessary permissions from principals and school districts. We conducted 14 case studies to generate data for the cross-site analysis.

Our sample includes the largest and one of the smallest school districts in the state. Other characteristics of the sample are delineated in Figure 1. Projects represented ranged from simple to complex, and focused on areas from reading or physical education to special services for handicapped or disruptive students. We also selected projects to represent different geographical areas of the state. Eight projects were in the Willamette Valley, which contains the bulk of the state's population, while the remaining six projects were in other areas.

FIGURE 1
Distribution of Mini Case Study Sites

District Type	Level of School			Total
	Elementary	Middle	High	
Urban	1	2	3	6
Suburban	2	-	-	2
Rural	3	2	1	6
Total	6	4	4	14

CROSS SITE ANALYSIS

Perhaps the most troublesome aspect of methodology for this study was the determination of how to organize information from the separate sites into meaningful patterns. We decided to have the two principal investigators do a content analysis of three case studies independently. They were to identify:

1. examples of behaviors exhibited by principal or members of the administrative team and seen as helpful by principal, project staff, or teachers;

22

2. examples of behaviors seen as essential to the success of the project; ones which administrators, project personnel, and teachers through would be critical to a project's success, even though those behaviors were not exhibited specifically in their project;
3. examples of unhelpful behaviors exhibited by principal or administrative team members and mentioned by principal, project staff, or teachers;
4. examples of content and processes recommended for inservice activities for principals;
5. problems, constraints, and opportunities affecting inservice options for principals.

The independent content analyses of these first cases were compared to determine inter-judge reliability. Since these analyses were reasonably similar, the remaining cases were distributed between the two investigators for a single reading. The first several "sorts" were done without the advance organization of a conceptual framework. Later, groups of like behaviors with a descriptor were compared with various conceptual schemes. Among these schemes were: (1) management functions (planning, organizing, motivating, controlling), (2) stages of educational change (initiating, incorporating, implementing, etc.), and (3) organization development concepts (role clarification, norms, communication channels, and the like).

The impetus for this book, then, is our own desire to discover—and to communicate to others—more effective ways of providing inservice education to administrators to help them with the critical tasks in their schools. Our examination of the literature and our own experience convinced us that there did not exist trustworthy descriptions of what principals actually do, or fail to do, that affects the fate of externally funded projects.

With a small grant from Teacher Corps, we conducted fourteen mini case studies to gather the empirical evidence we felt was needed as a basis for useful and appropriate recommendations about inservice. We then selected the eleven cases described in Chapter 2; the remaining three cases did not substantially add to the information in the cases we report.

Chapter 2 describes the eleven most informative of those cases, including the setting of the project, what it was all about, and how the principal's behavior affected its outcomes. Chapter 3 is a summary and analysis of those cases, presenting our findings about four discernable stages in the life cycles of projects and eight kinds of principal behaviors that seemed to have the greatest effect on the projects. Chapter 4 is addressed to principals and contains our recommendations; it identifies the issues about which decisions must be made in managing projects, the behaviors that help increase a project's chances for success, and the skills needed by principals for effective project management. Chapter 5, addressed primarily to staff development specialists and others who provide inservice education for administrators, presents our recommendations for the design and delivery of that inservice.

Our hope is that principals will find in these pages tools that will help them manage projects in their schools and that inservice providers will find guidelines for more effective inservice education. We also hope that funders of special projects such as we studied will attend more closely to the needs of the principal, who is responsible for spending their money wisely to bring about more productive and satisfying teaching and learning in our schools.

CHAPTER 2

Getting Down to Cases

We conducted fourteen mini case studies. In this chapter we present data on the eleven cases that we found most informative in describing how principals' behaviors affected externally funded projects. The cases represent a broad range of situations. We visited one of Oregon's largest schools and one of its smallest. We observed projects in both rural and urban settings. The projects dealt with a variety of innovations in reading programs, curriculum reform, special education, and community involvement. Some had strong community support, while others were received with disinterest or objections. Some were distinctly successful, while others were failures. And the principals varied widely in their support of their projects and their leadership styles, roles, and behaviors.

We present the cases here so that readers can have before them the evidence that we used to draw our conclusions about how principels operate with their schools and projects. In Chapter 3 we present our interpretation of the evidence given in these cases in the form of answers to the following questions which the reader may wish to keep in mind while going through the cases:

1. What leadership styles did these principals use? How were these styles appropriate—or inappropriate—to the expectations of staff and the needs of the project?

2. What roles did these principals play in their projects? What different functions did they serve?

3. What behaviors of principals seemed particularly helpful or unhelpful? That is, what actions facilitated the accomplishment of project goals and which seemed to restrain or hinder the project and its staff?
4. With what groups did the principal have the greatest influence and impact? In interactions with project staff? With central office and administrators? With students? With school board members?

FORMAT

The description of each case[1] is presented here in eight sections:

Prefatory observations.—Special attributes of the case, such as an unusual community, a noteworthy project, a remarkably effective or ineffective principal, or a highly representative set of issues.

The Community.—Highlights of the environment, including relationships between school and community; population and economic base, influences from nearby political, social, economic, or educational institutions; and other important community characteristics.

The Project.—The project's objectives, funding, population served, changes required of staff, and its history up to the time of the study.[2]

The Principal's Role in the Project.—The project staff's, faculty's, and principal's perceptions of the role played by the principal in the project. In one case in a small school, the administrative official held the title of "head teacher" rather than principal.

Facilitating Behaviors.—What a principal did—or should do—to help the project, as reported by the principal and others.

---

[1]All identifying names used in these descriptions—of people, schools, and communities—are pseudonyms. We hope we have sufficiently disguised the cases so that our promises of confidentiality have been kept.

[2]Interviews were conducted in spring of 1979 and the case studies were written from that time perspective.

Restraining Behaviors.—What kinds of actions by the principal were unhelpful or damaging to a project.

Inservice Training Needs.—Principals' and others' perceptions of administrators' needs for inservice training to help them support and manage externally funded projects.

Interpretations and Implications.—Reflections about the situation, generalizations drawn from comments and observations, ideas about how things might have been done differently, and important questions raised by the case.

CASE ONE
An Administrative Entrepreneur

In this case, we see the effect of a highly motivated and influential principal on the success of the school's project. Although the community is not thriving, the school stands as a symbol of optimism and caring, and the project reflects the energy, purpose, thoughts, skills, and behaviors of the principal.

THE COMMUNITY

Adjacent to a large metropolitan area, the town is accessible by means of a busy thoroughfare lined with bars, fast-food restaurants, and small businesses. Recent freeway construction has displaced homes and businesses. Vacant lots and recent construction line the road as one approaches the school.

The school appears well cared for, though it is in a neighborhood of small, run-down homes. It is a twenty-year-old, one-story building with a circular driveway, prominently placed flagpole, planter boxes of bedding plants, and freshly mowed grass.

The attention of a visitor entering the school is attracted to a large painting of the school's namesake, an early custodian in the district. Bulletin boards in the halls and office are bright and attractive. Children's art is displayed everywhere.

The office of principal Joe Lyons is bright, cheerful, and filled with children's art and notes to him. He has been at the school ten years. An athletic-looking fiftyish man, he was

27

casually dressed for the interview in sport shirt and slacks. He was attentive, enthusiastic, and apparently unrushed despite a constant babble of activity from the outer office.

He described how he began as an administrator 26 years ago. "One Sunday afternoon I got a phone call from the superintendent, and he asked if I'd like to try a new job. I said sure, why not? And I've been principal ever since."

Lyons noted that this school is considered the most difficult and poorest of the ten in the district: many of its 300 students are from low-income families. There is a large turnover in enrollment, and many children are eligible for the free lunch and breakfast program for low-income students. The staff has 12 teachers, a part-time specialist who assists with mainstreamed handicapped students, two CETA employees, a librarian and aide, the secretary, cafeteria help, and a custodian.

THE PROJECT

Since he took such an active role in the project, it seems appropriate to let Lyons' own words describe its beginning:

> I remember having a beer with a friend last winter. We were talking about the reading program we did here last summer and how the kids loved it and so did the teachers. My friend is a public relations man for a major oil company, and he mentioned that his company had given money for worthy projects in the past. That gave me an idea. What I did was write a two-page letter to that company asking for money to support a summer reading program. I said that our school was a low-income one, and the kids here lost as much as a year in reading level over the summer. What I wrote must have impressed them, because within a month I had received a check for $2500. I guess it helps to know someone, too.

Lyons then began to develop support for the program; he likened his methods to planting seeds. At a faculty meeting or social gathering he was likely to ask, "What do you think of this idea?" He would then describe an idea for a summer reading program so the group could develop it. A teacher described his method as using the faculty as a sounding board for new ideas.

28

By the time the project was funded, a group of interested teachers had formed. With the business manager's assistance, a way to funnel the money through the school's petty cash fund was found, which simplified paperwork and made hiring of summer staff easier. Teachers who had expressed interest in the program were interviewed and a staff of two teachers, several aides, and some parent volunteers was selected.

Specifics of the five-week program were planned by the summer school staff and the 26 children who attended. Preliminary planning was done in a series of brainstorming sessions involving the principal and participating teachers. One of the teachers described the process: "Mr. Lyons participated, but mainly to fill in details. He wanted us to do the planning, and we did. Mr. Lyons helped us set up the bus transportation and he went around to all classes to get support, but other than that, we planned it."

In the program, children took at least one major field trip a week, to the zoo, mountains, downtown, and the beach. These trips were documented with photos, drawings, and stories, which became part of "A Summer Journal," the final product. Other activities included reading and language arts activities, and planning for subsequent events.

THE PRINCIPAL'S ROLE IN THE PROJECT

In describing the principal's role in the project, one teacher said, "He's really concerned with kids, and always has ideas on how to help them. He likes to sound out his ideas with us, and then we can add and change and adapt."

Perhaps because of his inclusive approach, the principal's role was described by himself and his staff in strikingly similar terms. His role changed with each new stage in the project's life, and it also differed when he was dealing with internal or external audiences. He tended to let teachers take the leading role after the initial stages, but he was far more aggressive in his external impact. Figure 2 shows the different roles Lyons played.

29

FIGURE 2
Internal and External Impact of the Principal in Case 1

Phase	Internal (teachers or children in the school)	External (funders, parents, Central Office)
Preliminary (before project starts)	"Idea-planting" at social and faculty meetings; "What do you think of trying to start a summer reading program?"	Aggressive money finding; beer with a friend leads to a letter to potential funders and resulting check
Orientation	Building a group to plan: "Who'd like to participate?" "Let's get together and brainstorm."	Facilitating salaries through petty cash arrangement with Central Business Office; presenting and selling idea (and check) to superintendent and other principals; public relations
Planning	Hires "critical mass" group and gives them permission to plan and organize	Public relations with parents and rest of district
Implementation	Participates as a helper: ready to assist if difficulties arise	Public relations
Culmination	Hosts wrap-up barbeque; edits "A Summer Journal"	Makes sure project has visibility; everyone is thanked for helping

The school effectively created and implemented the summer reading program. The program's success and the way it was operated reflected the principal's style of leadership. He believed strongly in mutual expectations, group agreements, and participatory decision-making, and he seemed able to put his beliefs into action. Lyons described his role during implementation as advisor and helper if problems should arise. According to his and teachers' reports, some of his roles at this stage were bus driver, downtown tour guide, tent-pole setter and camp cook, and public relations specialist with central office staff and parents.

His role became more managerial and directive as the project concluded. He took responsibility for editing the "Summer Journal." He planned and hosted the culminating barbeque for participants, central office staff, parents, and funders, at which the Journal was distributed to all. He also wrote the Journal dedication:

> This book is dedicated to all boys and girls. I hope they will find reading a fun activity. The authors of stories are students from Crescent school, and are ages six through twelve. Stories and illustrations are the original work of these students. You will find some in their own handwriting and others typed. My special thanks to these children and the teachers who made this a worthwhile summer experience.

FACILITATING BEHAVIORS

It is clear that Lyons' self-perceived role was to stimulate and facilitate growth and change in his school. Throughout the interviews he emphasized the importance of collegial, participatory planning; so did the teachers who were interviewed. Lyons described his view of leadership in terms of mutual expectations: principals should "define what they expect and then assist teachers to live up to expectations."

He identified three decision situations in his school. In the first, there is no choice, and everyone must comply; his examples in this category were decisions on district-wide policy. In the second category, principals must make the decisions, as in hiring and firing situations. Most decisions in Crescent School are made the third way, by faculty consensus. He described the typical faculty meeting as one in which, after discussion and decision, he asks each participant, "Can you live with the decision?" He felt the wording was important because it reflects the mutual sharing that is important at his school.

Another part of his leadership effectiveness lay in his attention to individual differences among staff members: "A principal needs to know how to deal with different personalities and get the most out of them. Some teachers need kids to sit in rows, but an administrator can try to change the capabilities of teachers. You should try to get teachers to work to their strengths, to avoid their weaknesses."

31

RESTRAINING BEHAVIORS

The principal and staff identified very few restraining behaviors by the principal. The overall approval of the behaviors of the principal lets us infer that the reverse of the facilitating behaviors they identified would be detrimental to a project.

The View of the Principal.—Lyons had a hard time sorting out negative or unhelpful things he might have done. He did note, however, three possible problems within the project: all staff members were not involved, there was a certain amount of central office jealousy about the grant and about the success of the project, and the bookkeeping procedures could have been a problem.

The View of the Staff. —One teacher noted that it is a hindrance if the principal is not on staff when the project begins. It is also no help when the principal does not trust teachers and when he or she has too much input and an authroitarian planning style.

INSERVICE TRAINING NEEDS

Lyons and the teachers had similar comments about useful areas of training for principals. As may be expected, their comments stressed as essential the kinds of interpersonal and group process skills that Lyons demonstrated.

Lyons believed the central office in his district to be rather conservative in planning inservice for administrators. He would like to see an aggressive, comprehensive program of inservice that would stress group process skills, resource finding and proposal writing, supervision, and comprehensive curriculum development. He would prefer a retreat format or other time-off period for group reflection, problem-solving, and thinking.

Both teachers interviewed thought training for administrators should be essentially the same as that for teachers regarding content. They placed high value on trust, openness and communication skills, resource knowledge, and Glasser-type training for principals and teachers alike.

Schedule flexibility is more available to principals and thus more creative training formats could be developed for them. Teachers are more restricted to after-class times. Both Lyons and the teachers reported an opportunity they had had last year to fly to another state to observe an open school. This visit led to some structural and management changes at Crescent School and seemed an effective inservice method.

INTERPRETATIONS AND IMPLICATIONS

Participatory planning was crucial to the success of this reading project, and there is evidence that participation is the customary style of decision-making at the school. The principal believes in high levels of trust and mutual expectations for staff and children. In Crescent School, this approach seems to be an effective way to build school pride, group cohesiveness, and a readiness to try change. The contrast between the rundown neighborhood and Crescent School, with its manicured lawns and fresh flowers in the office, was dramatic. Equally dramatic was the sense of purpose and optimism that was so obvious in Lyons' conversations and in the comments of the teachers. The faculty has not been restricted by its surroundings and has brought a creative and innovative summer program to a group of low-income nonachievers.

The principal says that he likes Crescent School because of its low-income setting: he feels challenged by the number of reluctant learners and turned-off students, and his hope is to find a way to stimulate these children to more positive feelings about themselves and school.

The positive, active optimism observed at this school reflects Lyons' faith in his staff, his high expectations for their ability to plan, and his entrepreneurship in actively seeking money to finance innovation.

The success of this innovation was clearly due to a unique individual, Mr. Lyons. He was able to combine the aggressive money-getting entrepreneur role with "stand back and let them plan it" participatory decision-making. He facilitated resources and provided support throughout the project, from dealing with the business office to pounding tent stakes. His

33

vision and personal style are what made this program a success. Mr. Lyons appeared able to sense which leadership role—authoritarian, aggressive, supportive, advocate, or facilitator—was most appropriate to his audience and to the particular phase of implementation.

If the skills Lyons demonstrated can be taught, there is a clear message for inservice education in this case. Lyons' behavior was effective because it was appropriate to the particular situation, stage of implementation, and audience with whom he was dealing. One possibility for inservice is to find ways of teaching that sensitivity and those skills; training would include both skills of diagnosing the situation to know what action is appropriate and building the principal's repertoire of styles and actions to match the situation. It could also be useful to find other administrators with this natural feel for implementation, to give them further training, and to then set up model implementation sites for less skillful implementers to visit. The school shows that the situation and resources are important, but not in the usual sense of quantity and quality. Here, where money is tight and conservatively managed, and students are poor, the entrepreneurship of the principal in finding a creative source of funds spurred district-wide interest in creating change.

CASE TWO
Moving Backstage:
A Principal's Approach to Successful Innovation

The principal in this case had two very clear ideas about how to install an innovation in his school. He thought people had to understand in advance what roles people played in the project to achieve its objectives and he thought staff had to take over the effort as soon as possible. How he put those ideas into action and what happened as a result are the core of this narrative. The impact of the experience on all project personnel is reflected in their views of what kind of inservice education for principals would be valuable in enhancing innovation.

34

One of the early settlements in Oregon Territory, this town has aged well, maintaining some of its historical flavor while keeping quiet pace with the region's economic growth. In recent years it has become the suburb of a nearby city. But at the same time, it has its own strong economic base in agriculture and in the mills.

The downtown area suffers a bit from the crowding dictated by topography and still boasts many of the old stone Victorian structures that graced its early streets. A railroad runs through its center, adding to the congestion. In recent decades, much of the town's economic activity has spread out along the highways leading into the countryside and connecting it with the small rural communities for which it provides various services. Between the arms of this sprawling business district are acre after acre of fairly recent middle-income homes.

This is the county seat, another reason for considerable activity. The busy streets include farmers in town to sell produce or buy supplies, residents transacting business, salesmen and buyers from national business concerns, housewives doing a bit of routine shopping, and mill and supply-house workers changing shifts.

The school system had to begin to expand about fifteen years ago, leading to the building of two junior high schools and several elementary schools. A new, airy, wooden administration building houses the district's superintendent, several curriculum specialists, and the clerical staff.

The junior high school studied, which serves some 500 students, was built eleven years ago in the midst of fields a bit beyond the edge of town. The halls sport broad bands of color and imaginative lettering to direct students to the cafeteria, industrial arts wing, home economics wing, social studies, etc. The effect is lively and upbeat. The atmosphere of the school reflects enthusiasm and apparent attention to the business of education—along with clothes, boys, girls, sports, and whatever else occupies the thirteen- and fourteen-year-old mind.

35

The project is a federally funded exemplary program in career education, integrating career information and basic skills into the basic curriculum begun at the school three years ago. The project replaces separate classes devoted to career education, which both students and teachers found uninspiring. Teaching about careers is now done by all teachers, regardless of subject area, as part of the regular curriculum. For example, students in English classes may learn to fill out application forms and write letters of application, math students may solve problems involving salaries and payrolls, and a social studies unit may include information on careers associated with that topic of study. At the end of ninth grade, students who have completed nine of eleven specified steps earn academic credit toward graduation.

The project emphasizes exploration and career awareness, leaving specific choices and vocational skills training to high school. It also presents a wide variety of information to students for expanding that awareness, and combines career possibilities and academic curriculum in ways that have more meaning for students than did the separate career education classes.

An important focus of the project is a Career Day near the end of the school year, when people from twenty to thirty occupations make presentations to students in small sessions. A student prepares during the year to choose the three or four presentations of most interest to him or her. Thus, by graduation each student will have listened to as many as twelve discussions by people in occupations in which the student has an interest. Students can then make the necessary choices of training during high school to improve the chances of making satisfying career selections.

Seven people were interviewed about the project and the principal's role in it: the district specialist, the principal, and five teachers, one of whom is the building coordinator for the project.

This project—coordinated by a career education specialist

in the central office—was originally initiated (successfully) in another school in the district. Neither principal Paul Harrison nor the specialist remembers precisely who took the initiative to bring it into this school. Both think the decision grew out of their discussions and dissatisfaction with the existing program. Within the school the initial decision was the principal's: he wrote the proposal that requested the project, and he and the specialist planned the steps needed to initiate it.

Two abortive attempts to win the faculty's support were made before a third approach proved successful. All three began with an inservice training event, but the first two were the traditional kind of inservice for college credit and were met with a total lack of enthusiasm by the staff. Reasons cited for their failure were that the training required additional time from the staff, they were presented as "packages" that teachers were expected to accept, and the staff saw that implementation would require yet more work from them. The principal and specialist agree that the last reason was probably the most damaging. Interestingly, none of the staff interviewed remembers the first two presentations.

The third presentation, this one successful, tried a new tack. Teachers were taken, department by department, for a planning day away from the building. They were given lunch and charged with completing planning for the new program that they had begun a month before. During that month they had worked in groups of two or three with the principal, the district career specialist, and another specialist from the State Department of Education. That planning, done in low-key fashion during teachers' free periods, had made extensive use of the skills and experience of each teacher. It was based on clear guidelines, was worked out in careful detail by the principal, and had as its goal the final planning day away from the school.

The planning day was held at the local country club, simply because room was available there. This site, chosen for expediency, became an important bonus. The country club setting signaled that teachers were being recognized as professionals, their contributions requested, and their opinions valued. The "specialness" of the setting and arrangements brought home to them the importance of what they were being asked to do.

THE PRINCIPAL'S ROLE IN THE PROJECT

The View of the Principal.—Harrison remembered a long period of careful planning and preparation of materials that teachers would need to carry out their planning. Their active involvement overlapped his own only for about a month; as they took over and elected their own coordinator, he stepped back.

Elaborate materials had been developed by the principal and the district specialist in preparation for the teachers' planning. These included—for the first time—a chart of all course offerings in the school, presented in such a way that goals and objectives of the new career education program could be added in appropriate curriculum areas. This detailed matrix was later adopted by the district and is being extended to all grade levels to coordinate the district's curriculum offerings.

One goal of the planning day was the selection of a building coordinator for the project. Following this selection, the principal no longer spearheaded the operation of the project, and the new curriculum became a reality in the school.

The View of the Staff.—Both teachers and principal were in agreement that the principal's support is essential to the project. Teachers were for the most part unaware of the extent of the principal's involvement prior to their entry into the project, but recognized that his leadership was a key factor in their success with their own planning from that point on. They remembered that his leadership was strong and forceful in keeping efforts focused on goals and in maintaining cohesion among the staff, while the actual planning and implementation of the project were theirs.

FACILITATING BEHAVIORS

The View of the Principal.—The principal saw both his extensive planning and his deliberate stepping back from project leadership as essential to the program's success and to good administration. The planning assured that teachers would have a clear structure within which to work out their individual contributions, with the materials at hand that they needed. Stepping back, once the complex coordination of getting the entire staff under way together was done, allowed the staff to assume responsibility for the activities of the project and for attaining its goals. The principal removed himself almost entirely from operation of the project, but kept fully informed of activities, plans, and developments by the coordinator, and still retains financial responsibility for equipment and materials needs.

The role change was necessary on two levels, Harrison felt, for a school of this size. First, it allowed the project to become the property of the staff, rather than an imposed undertaking with which they must comply, a step that is essential to both staff morale and the success of the project. Those benefits were enhanced by the creation of the leadership role of the building coordinator, a fellow staff member who can be approached freely with concerns a teacher may have.

The other reason for the role change for the principal was the size and complexity of the school's administrative demands. The principal felt he needed to be free of the more time-consuming operational details of any one program to coordinate all the school's programs. The project's teacher management was only one of many management responsibilities assumed voluntarily by individual teachers. This delegation of authority, even to the hiring of new staff members by committees of teachers, freed the principal from overwhelming demands on his time and assured that the staff developed ownership of all aspects of the school and its operation. It was an important ingredient of the high morale noted in the school.

The View of the Staff.—The principal was seen by most of the staff as strong, capable, kind, purposeful, methodical, and, for the most part, democratic. His insistence on clearly defined roles and goals in all endeavors and his encouragement of staff

39

members to assume leadership in the school's many non-curricular activities resulted in an unusual degree of participation by the faculty in all aspects of the school's operation.

One staff member felt that the strong role assumed by the principal in laying the groundwork for teacher acceptance, and in steering the various departments in the same direction as project planning was developed within each of them, accounted to a large extent for the notable success of the project.

RESTRAINING BEHAVIORS

The View of the Principal.—While the principal did not explicitly identify administrative actions he considered detrimental to a project, reasonable inferences about his beliefs can be drawn from his actions. He would probably say that two sources of trouble were a failure to delegate authority and transfer ownership in the project, and a failure to clearly identify roles and goals.

The View of the Staff.—While a small faction saw the principal as cool and aloof, unresponsive to their needs, most saw him as responsive, supporting, and democratic. Even those who saw him as at times unyielding and tactless believed that he put the interests of students first; second place was shared by his own interests and those of the teachers and the district.

Implicit in these comments is a belief that a principal assists a project by being supportive, responsive, and democratic. One staff member explained that problems have emerged that may be due in part to what is seen by some as a somewhat autocratic streak in the principal when interests among staff conflict or when larger interests of the school seem to conflict with desires of individual staff members.

INSERVICE TRAINING NEEDS

The View of the Principal.—Harrison expressed a desire for a variety of exchange opportunities—for both teachers and principals—with other schools and with business and industry. He would like to bring representatives of businesses known to have outstanding operations into the school's classrooms to help bring more meaning to the academic and career education ingredients of the curriculum.

As to training for an innovative project, he would like to make this same kind of exchange with a school which has been successful in the management of an innovation. That exchange would allow him to observe that program and would allow the other principal to offer suggestions, based on his own success, that he felt would be useful in this school. Its value, he felt, would go far beyond the simple exchange of information or a simulation that one finds in an inservice workshop. The direct experience allows absorption on various levels of many kinds of information and responses to the real situation. However, again, he would not restrict this experience to principals: he felt teachers could benefit equally from working briefly with another system and understanding how and why it works.

The View of the Staff.—Since most of the teachers interviewed expressed contentment with the principal's leadership, they identified administrators' inservice needs as those which would promote the qualities they like in him. Training to improve communication skills was considered a basic need by teachers, as was training in basic management skills and in understanding a variety of managerial styles, so that a principal could shift from one to another as appropriate.

Since those skills were felt to be essential both to the success of the project and to the overall success of the school, staff members saw no separate training needs that were specific to the management of an innovative project.

INTERPRETATIONS AND IMPLICATIONS

In this fairly large, recently built suburban junior high school with a middle-class attendance, an innovation was—after some difficulties—integrated into the curriculum and has proved highly successful.

Credit for that success was seen by all as due to the staff's enthusiastic participation. Credit for that participation, in turn, was generally given to the principal: for his strong leadership, early clarification of goals and roles, careful advance planning, and delegation of authority and responsibility for the daily operation of the project to the staff and their elected representative in the final phase of planning. That delegation was not seen by most staff members as a lack of support or interest, but rather as a willingness to allow them to run their own program. He saw himself—and they saw him—as facilitator and motivator and then as supporter.

CASE THREE

Insight and Skills: Keys to a Project's Success

The principal in this study has been highly successful in introducing and supporting innovative projects. Listening to what he has come to believe is important in his role, and how project staff responded to his actions provides a fascinating overview of effective change in schools. As in the first two cases, this principal followed a strategy of an early, strong leadership role followed by a delegation of authority and responsibility for the project to the staff.

THE COMMUNITY

This city—the largest in the state—has won numerous awards for quality of living. Its economy is based on wood products and "clean" industries such as electronics and tourism. The city has had modest population growth in the past decade, but the school population has stabilized and some schools have experienced modest enrollment declines.

The school district has experienced many of the problems found in most urban districts—teacher unrest, conflict over busing and desegregation, decentralization, and budget defeats. Generally, however, the community has supported education and the district has a good reputation for the quality of its instructional program.

Central Elementary School, the major site for the project, is in a predominately white, middle-class neighborhood in the southwest part of the city. Built more than sixty years ago, the building has had two additions in the past thirty years. The old brick building and landscaped grounds boast bright colors and pleasant, well-kept conditions.

The school has an enrollment of about 380 students and a staff of approximately 24. Until a year ago, enrollment was larger and included grades 7 and 8, which were moved to a new middle school. Central has fifteen permanent classrooms, a portable classroom used for special subjects, a cafeteria, and a gym. Besides the Title IV-C project described in this study, there are also special programs in instrumental music and speech therapy, and special services for children with extreme learning problems and those who are emotionally handicapped.

THE PROJECT

A program in which gifted students tutor handicapped students, the Title IV-C project was at Central and two nearby elementary schools. As described in a continuation proposal, the project's mission was "to develop a transportable differentiated model for exceptional children in grades K–6 which will result in those children's having a more positive attitude toward themselves, others, and school."

The project's strategy was to identify handicepped and gifted children and their attitudes toward themselves, others, and school. These children received special instruction aimed at improving their attitudes by providing them with outlets to challenge their abilities and by channeling their interests toward self-enrichment, production of knowledge, and awareness of others.

Funded at $60,000 per year, the project was in its second year when we visited it. Most of the funds supported two full-time professionals and a part-time secretary. One professional had considerable experience in materials development and was recruited from a local university for the project. The other, an expert in education of the gifted, was selected after a national search for a person who understood education of the gifted and also had demonstrated effectiveness in working with both gifted and handicapped students. Both appeared to be capable professionals who were extremely enthusiastic about the project.

43

Martin Lawrence is an experienced administrator who has been principal of Central since 1975. He has been in the district five years as a teacher and twenty-five years as a principal, and has worked in seven schools.

In the interview, he was a reflective, soft-spoken man, given to understatement. On several occasions he said he was not sure how much help he could be in the research effort; but he usually followed that disclaimer with very insightful and penetrating ideas about change in schools, the principal's role in that effort, and the inservice he had found helpful.

Lawrence was the primary person in identifying the problem addressed by the project and in getting the project funded. He began his efforts during his first year as principal at Central. From a study of test scores and from listening to comments by parents and teachers, he concluded that the school had many students who were gifted and talented; he thought a special program was needed to serve them.

Three years before our study he had held a series of meetings with parents and teachers to discuss the problem. In what he called "low key" awareness and planning sessions, the groups planned for a possible project and explored potential funding sources.

Those initial activities were followed up in 1976/77 when a group of teachers, with Lawrence's assistance, decided to submit a proposal to the State Department of Education, ESEA Title IV-C. The project received a favorable nod from the department and the principal and a new resource person hired with project funds started more formal planning and development work during 1977/78.

As reported by Lawrence and project personnel, his involvement during the first year of the project was very intense. He said he attended meeting after meeting with various interested groups in the school, with parents, and with the "state people." Title IV-C required that the first year of the project be devoted to planning; Lawrence, during this time, was getting input from various groups that would lead to his rewriting of the original proposal.

The principal and the resource person also decided during the planning year that two full-time resource teachers or specialists would be needed—one to head up product and materials development, the other to serve more as a teacher with face-to-face contact with students. He convinced personnel in the central office to allow him to conduct a national search for project staff, something not normally done in this district. The search produced an applicant from another state who had a national reputation in education of the gifted. She joined the project for the 1978/79 school year.

Lawrence reported that his intense involvement with the project decreased greatly after that time. In his words, he "had found two extremely competent people to run the project and my role should now be one of supporting their activities." He also admitted that some of his energy was drained away from the project when he had to implement a district decision to create middle schools.

FACILITATING BEHAVIORS

Staff members interviewed had nothing but glowing comments about the support and encouragement that Lawrence gave the project. Even probes to find weaknesses produced favorable comments.

Project personnel believed that the project got off to a good start mainly because of the many, many meetings that Lawrence had held with parents and teachers prior to submitting a proposal. Even though many of the goals and activities of the project have changed drastically since those early discussions, the meetings seemed, according to project staff, to gain commitment for the project by a fairly large group of parents and teachers. Also, the principal was able to get resources from the district to hire a five-teacher writing team during the summer to prepare the proposal for submission.

Both project staff and the principal reported that a primary role he played was supervising proposal preparation and negotiating the budget, determining the scope of work, and reconciling differences in expectations between project participants and the funding agency. Project staff said, "Not only is he supportive to the project, he's an old hand at this type of thing." Lawrence had had many funded projects in his buildings; as he talked about earlier projects, it became clear that his strategy had remained consistent over the years. It included getting a group of people to discuss some mutually identified problem, searching for outside resources, obtaining grant monies, and then hiring qualified personnel to carry out the project.

Although Lawrence never spoke of it, project staff mentioned again and again his willingness to run interference for them with the central office and his willingness to acquire resources and support at the district level. They saw him as a person who knew his way around the district and who had the trust and support of high-level administrators. They said, "he can get on the phone and speak to the right people" without being shuffled from office to office as they sometimes were.

This project required support from parents and teachers for its success. Parents had to agree on the procedures used to identify the gifted and they had to provide links to the larger community. All involved had to endorse the concept of gifted students' serving as tutors to handicapped students. Teachers needed to be willing to have students leave their classrooms for special instruction and to provide follow-up activities. The project called for considerable inservice training for teachers and for some parent aides to be held outside the regular school day. Project staff saw the principal as being the critical factor in getting teachers to attend the inservices—not because he told them they had to, but because he gave strong verbal support to the project and did everything he could to arrange the schedule to make the time more acceptable to participants. He also attended every inservice event; project staff reported that he modelled good participant behaviors, such as being active, taking the training seriously, and encouraging others to do the same.

46

Lawrence also seemed to excel at explaining the project's goals and requirements to others, in part because he understood the nature of the project. Title IV-C projects aim not only at improving some aspect of the pilot school but also at developing materials and practices that can be applied elsewhere. It is often difficult to explain to taxpayers why their monies are supporting things that will be used elsewhere, to parents why their children should serve as "guinea pigs" in an experimental project, and to teachers why some people seem to have a lot of time to write and think instead of instructing students all day.

The project staff again and again reported that Lawrence was a man with "high energy" and one who had better abilities than anyone else they had ever worked with to reach out and acquire outside resources. They reported that he actively recruited student teachers and actively recruited parent aides and community volunteers. As one project staff member put it, "Whereas some administrators are afraid to have outside people in the building, Lawrence grabs on to anyone he sees if he thinks it will add to the school's instructional program."

INSERVICE TRAINING NEEDS

No special training for principals was provided in this project, and the principal was already well versed in initiating and managing change projects. It is clear, though, that inservice events he had experienced over the years had served him well.

Asked what kinds of inservice experiences he had found most useful, Lawrence named several. First, he said that he had learned to write well in college and that he thought that this skill was of considerable assistance in his abilities to get projects funded. Second, he thought he had good group discussion skills. He was able to get groups of people to sit down and, in his words, "brainstorm ideas." He also thought he was able to get groups of people to "package an idea" in a format that was understandable to funders and clients.

As to specific inservice events that stood out in Lawrence's memory, he noted three that occurred during the late sixties.

47

First, he went through a series of training events between 1967 and 1969. They were a clinic in sensitivity training conducted by the staff of a university medical school, several leadership training seminars conducted by a staff development specialist from a local electronics firm, and group process workshops conducted by a regional educational laboratory. He said all were good in giving him understanding and skills for "working with people," which he saw as prerequisite for running a successful project.

Lawrence also reported that he had attended "hundreds" of inservice events during his thirty years as an educator. Many, he reported, were failures. He described as important to the success of inservice for principals: the quality of the instructors, the time that the inservice is held (he agrees with his teachers that he doesn't like to work after school or on Saturdays), and the timing and substance of the inservice—it shouldn't be spread out over too long a period of time and it should get down to what is relevant for "day-to-day work."

INTERPRETATIONS AND IMPLICATIONS

Martin Lawrence in many ways appears to be a model for how principals should provide leadership to an externally funded project. From watching the way he took the initiative in recognizing the need for the project and in defining the problem, as well as the way in which he provided leadership to other persons involved in the project, we can learn a great deal about helpful roles of the principal.

Of particular interest is Lawrence's role in dealing with the many groups whose interests, values, and resources are relevant to a project. He got staff members involved, negotiated with the funding agency, explained the project to parents, and "ran interference" at the central office to help smooth the project's way. Those actions direct attention to the roles we will later identify as "linker," "liaison," "resource acquirer," and negotiator. Given the limited amount of time a principal can devote to any one segment of his or her school—such as a project—decisions must be made about how that time should

48

be spent. Lawrence's answer was to hire competent staff in whom he had confidence to handle the core tasks of the project, while he attended to tasks of linking the project with other important parts of the system.

Finally, we note that Lawrence felt his most important learnings from inservice training and other experiences were a writing ability and skills in involving others.

Success in a Very Small School

In rural areas there are very small schools in which a head teacher carries out the duties that fall to a principal in larger schools. This case describes how the head teacher with a faculty of only four—in a school limited by its remoteness and lack of services common to larger schools—assisted in introducing a new project into the school.

Three features of this study are especially noteworthy: the unanimity of views about how the head teacher operated throughout the project, the role changes she made in response to changing conditions, and her perceptions of appropriate inservice education for administrators.

THE COMMUNITY

This tiny community is like dozens of crossroads collections of sun-grayed, wind-roughened houses and shacks scattered across eastern Oregon. Two or three small old wooden houses and a dozen sheds cluster around the crossroads of the paved two-lane road stretching east and west, and the gravel road crossing it from north to south. Nothing else man-made shows across the sagebrush desert except a thin utility line and occasional wire fence. It's near enough to a state park to have occasional visitors from elsewhere; locally it's mostly noted for the only general store, gas station, post office, and public telephone for miles around. And hardly anybody lives there.

Most of its customers are ranchers trying to grow grain or raise cattle on land only recently cleared of sagebrush, though a handful of families have been here for several generations.

49

Some ranchers, with enough capital and hard work, are fairly prosperous. Many hopeful newcomers cannot make it and have to give up after a while to be replaced by a new set. There's some ranch work for wages but not much else for income. A commercial plant a few miles away employs a small work force, and a few other small enterprises hang on in the area, but possible employment is limited almost entirely to sporadic ranch work.

Down the side road a couple hundred yards sits the community's elementary (and only) school; high school students are bused out of town. Housed in prefab structures are four classrooms of two grades each. The old grade school building, a tiny neat wooden house at the edge of the school yard, is now used for storage and special projects. The classrooms in the new buildings are carpeted, light, open, and uncluttered. The atmosphere is pleasant and quiet.

Fewer than a hundred students are enrolled in the eight grades, some traveling 60 miles by bus each day. Although opportunity is limited and living is hard, the broad vistas of untilled sagebrush seem to beckon an increasing number of young families fleeing from the cities of California and western Oregon; the school population has nearly doubled in four years. This transcience of a growing proportion of the student body poses a major problem for the school.

This school is too small to merit a certified principal, and instead employs a head teacher, Pamela Bishop, who administers the school's business, supervises the other four teachers, and teaches two grades. There are no aides or secretaries; the only non-classroom staff is one part-time teacher who works individually with students who need special help.

The school staff left a strong impression of high morale and pride in their school, something of a surprise in this remote corner of the desert where the outsider might expect morale to slump under the dullness of routine and lack of stimulation. The atmosphere in the school was at once businesslike and warm.

A number of students were experiencing painful failures. Because they had come into the school with a fragmented educational background, their self-concept and motivation to learn were low.

The head teacher's strong ideas about the value of acquiring physical skills in the process of education coincided with the presentation the fall before our study of a new program made available by the Education Service District (ESD). (Small rural schools in Oregon are often dependent on the ESD— which is like a county or intermediate education district—for services.) In this case, the special projects director for the ESD presented a federally funded project for enhancing physical development to a number of county schools.

The project was based on the concept of "movement education." During the time usually allotted to traditional physical education classes (about 20 minutes per day in Oregon), students experienced a variety of activities, such as dance, exploring their physical environment, play. The activities were designed to make students use all major muscle groups in their bodies and to find out their individual physical capabilities.

The head teacher and her staff discussed the proposed project and decided to participate. She was enthusiastic about the program, because it matched her earlier teaching experience. But she believed the staff made the decision freely as a group, rather than because of pressure from her. The program was put into effect shortly after the beginning of the school year, about six months before the interview.

There were some mild reservations. One teacher was skeptical and felt that organized competitive sports might be threatened. Bishop shared that reservation, but wanted to give the program a chance. Both expressed relief that the program did not affect competitive sports or dull the enjoyment of those students who enjoyed them. All the staff agreed that the project had been good for the school, expressing their views of the results in such terms as: "students show increased imagi-

51

nation in other play activities, increased vocabulary and attention span in other subjects"; "each child participates actively and succeeds . . . not afraid of failure . . . more language facility, better attention"; "better body control, listening skills . . . shows up in reading and math."

THE HEAD TEACHER'S ROLE IN THE PROJECT

The View of the Head Teacher.—The head teacher described herself as "positive" about the project from the outset, and others concurred. Its focus matched the value she placed on non-competitive programs. Once her worries about its effect on competitive sports were relieved, she was enthusiastic. She felt that she was supportive and encouraging; the staff believed *they* made the decision to adopt the project. She thought she left the planning for implementation up to the staff; her role was one of facilitation and then of management. Initially the head teacher's role was one of promoter of the innovation. Once the tasks of initiating the project and running interference for it were done, her role changed to that of manager and facilitator. Actual planning and implementation were done by the three teachers directly involved in the project, while she remained highly supportive and responsive to expressed needs. Her role as advocate to the school board and community continued unchanged.

Her own assessment of her leadership style emphasized clarity, honesty, and a positive attitude, all of which were reflected in comments by her and the staff. She said she took the job "to see if I could take on a new challenge and do a good job of it." No one suggested that Bishop merely maintained a school already functioning at a high level of efficiency and morale. There were hints that things had greatly improved, but the kind of negative statement it would take to confirm that wouldn't be heard from her or her staff. Divisive influences in the community were frequently reflected in the school, but they had not undermined the strong sense of unity that prevailed.

The View of the Staff.—The head teacher's support role was

52

described by various teachers as taking whatever steps were requested to make it possible for them to carry out the program effectively. For example, she assisted, if asked, in discipline problems; she handled the administrative work necessary to assure adequate supplies when they were needed; and, not least important, she knew how the program was functioning in each classroom and took pains to tell her teachers how she felt they were doing.

Her teachers saw her as totally supportive. They credited her with anticipating needs for equipment and material and arranging for much of the basic equipment in advance. They felt they had latitude to work out their own systems of application, which varied considerably but with consistent results, but that she was there when needed.

How did other staff members see her leadership style?

- "Doesn't pressure, gives a free hand, is supportive of the teachers, keeps confidences, tries to build a person's feeling about himself . . . his self-image . . . is very positive . . . solves problems . . . willing to try new ideas . . . provides clear goals."
- "Very positive . . . very supportive, backs teachers . . . respects your privacy."
- "Gets things done . . . very concerned about your feelings . . . says what she means, you always know where you are with her."

She was a woman supervising two experienced men, as well as two other experienced women, and they were unanimous in their support of her policies and leadership practices. That no doubt reflected her staunch support of them; it also reflected her attention to their needs and her determination to make things run smoothly for all of them. She tried to anticipate needs and to plan in advance. She emphasized the importance of clarity of expectations and goals, and she took every opportunity to give positive feedback.

FACILITATING BEHAVIORS

The View of the Head Teacher.—The head teacher felt that a

53

positive attitude was essential to the morale of the school staff and important to the success of a special project.

The View of the Staff.—Without exception, all staff agreed that without the administrator's support it would be futile to carry out an innovation of any major scale. Too much coordinating, objective feedback, community clarification, and general management is needed, all of which fall normally to the principal.

The head teacher's role as mediator and conciliator between the school and the board was often cited as essential to the continuation of the program. She was credited with handling most of the criticisms of the program and with interpreting it to those who opposed it, even though some continuing resistance from some families was expected.

RESTRAINING BEHAVIORS

Neither head teacher nor staff had strong complaints about the project's implementation. In discussing difficulties that might have been better handled, staff members invariably mentioned aspects of the program rather behaviors of the head teacher. These difficulties were felt to be the entire staff's responsibility rather than problems that should have been anticipated by the head teacher.

Both the head teacher and the staff expressed regret about the fact that the head teacher did not attend either of two inservice activities offered by the ESD as training for this project, but the weight of the criticism was light indeed. Both Bishop and the teachers felt it would have been useful for the project if she had been able to attend, but as she put it, "someone had to stay here to mind the store." The feeling her staff expressed was that she managed the program very capably without this training, but her job no doubt would have been easier if she had got the information first-hand.

INSERVICE TRAINING NEEDS

The head teacher felt that principals would benefit from training that described the content and objectives of the project if they were not already familiar with them. She would have liked to receive inservice training in management skills and in handling discipline and budgets at the outset of her administrative duties. For county schools in particular, she suggested workshops in ESD resources and personnel. Obstacles to administrators' attendance at such training sessions, she felt, are fewer than for classroom teachers. In fact, she suggested that principals are often uninterested, "lazy," and perhaps more interested in the politics of the title than in improving education for children.

Bishop's own experience in attending numerous statewide inservice training sessions, as well as in conducting several, led her to believe that small-group sessions are more effective than one-to-one kinds of training in allowing exchange among participants. This then requires sponsorship by a larger agency—perhaps, in the case of county schools, the county ESD. Attention to three considerations could make inservice training particularly useful to administrators, in her opinion.

Financial assistance beyond the resources of the local school district for attendance at training sessions is a necessity for small districts. It could be made available through agencies such as the ESD.

A real need that she saw for administrators is classroom experience on a more regular basis than is usual for principals. She would like to see principals teaching at least six months out of every five to six years in order to remain in touch with the real purpose of the school, the education of children, and the needs of teachers.

Finally, she would like to see training directed toward the problems of small schools as apart from large schools.

INTERPRETATIONS AND IMPLICATIONS

Those behaviors which appear essential to the success of an innovative project are those directly related to leadership initially and to management later on. The initial leadership seems to require high visibility at the outset of the project but may diminish considerably to behind-the-scenes support as staff members assume responsibility for the project's operation. A probably essential behavior is the transfer of "ownership" to allow staff members to assume responsibility as the project develops. If the extent to which staff members feel the project is their own relates to its success, clearly the principal's leadership role must become less prominent.

Management, on the other hand, may be carried out with very low visibility—handling the mechanics of the project to "keep the machine oiled," seeing that problems are solved as they emerge, and supplying materials and services as needed. Visibility, following the initiation of the project, may only be useful in giving staff regular feedback. Their awareness of continuing support is a necessary ingredient to staff morale, but it may be accomplished quietly by letting staff members know that they are doing well and that, in a bind, immediate help is available.

In summary, the project's success was due in large part to the way the head teacher carried out project management. Her actions included winning full participation of the staff and assuring that support was given when it was needed. It also included allowing the teaching staff to assume as much responsibility for the project's success as they felt capable of, making it their project, not hers. It included protecting them and the project to some extent from community harassment, giving them freedom to function, and confirming her support of their undertaking. The smooth fit of the project into the normal operation of the school can also be attributed in large part to her management skills and to the receptive climate she helped establish.

Special inservice training for administrators that would promote the attitudes, communication skills, and management skills that have been cited as basic to this administrator's success with this project would clearly be valuable to administrators of other innovative projects. This training should be designed to clarify the goals and concepts of the project itself and to prepare the administrator for the role of advocate that the principal may need to fill with the staff and the community.

Watertown: The Past Confronts the Future

Watertown has had a varied history as a community, and the school in this study reflects the changes. The project here was intended to improve both the offerings and the image of the school to attract a more varied student population.

Some of the project staff had been in the school for years and they had strong preferences about how principals should operate. The challenge this situation offered the principal is one we can expect to find in more and more schools as faculties become more entrenched and include fewer fledgling teachers.

THE COMMUNITY

Watertown began as a settlement of railroad workers in the early 1900s. The community has seen hard times, but things are getting better. Young people are buying and remodelling older houses, and the school's "magnet" program is attracting a wider variety of socioeconomic levels. The district has reorganized and redrawn school boundary lines to help desegregate the system. Watertown, with an enrollment that is about half white and half minority, has the largest minority population in the district. A core of academically gifted students is emerging at the school.

The physical layout of the school includes a playing field to the south of a freshly painted main building. Declining enrollment has allowed the remodelling of several classrooms into large dance studios and other special-purpose rooms.

The faculty is extremely stable; a few teachers are themselves Watertown graduates. At the time of the interview, many wore buttons showing that they were among the 700 teachers picketing a school board meeting to demonstrate their seriousness about contract negotiations.

Watertown is a magnet school for the performing arts with an emphasis on dance, and its project is housed in a huge second-floor classroom divided by temporary partitions. For three years the state financed the project with funds for innovative projects; this past year—one of institutionalization—was funded by the district.

The project was part of a comprehensive plan that coupled the magnet school with massive curricular and organizational change. Major elements of the proposal were organizational restructuring, curriculum design, development of minimum competencies, community and feeder-school relationships, and evaluation.

Participatory decision-making and significant faculty responsibility for curriculum planning and implementation marked the project. A management team for the project consisted of the principal, curriculum vice-principal, project coordinator, unit leaders, heads of groups of teachers from subject areas, and program leaders who were comparable to department heads.

Following a district needs assessment in 1974, a faculty committee met to design a program to meet needs that were identified. A faculty member who was very interested in dance enthusiastically advocated a performing arts emphais for Watertown's magnet program. Despite some community concern about an "entertainer" stereotype in a magnet program for the school with the district's largest minority population, the staff hoped that the magnet school program would attract better students (the district has a voluntary busing program) and improve academic standards.

After the project's inception, two new administrators were brought into the school. People were unsure, during the project's first year, as to just what it was supposed to do, and they worried that funding from regular programs would be diverted to the magnet program.

The View of the Principal.—An impressive antique rolltop desk, obviously the pride of its owner, was prominently placed in the office of principal Bill Foster when we interviewed him. Very reflective about his leadership style, Foster pictured himself as relatively happy go lucky. He said, though, that he felt uncomfortable in unstructured situations, especially if he had a task responsibility; but he also felt distressed in a closely structured situation when no closure was near. One of his concerns about being principal was that he felt less free to say things he could say when he was a curriculum vice-principal or teacher.

He was one of the two administrators brought to the school in the fall of 1975, along with George Brennan, then the principal. Their leadership styles differed—Brennan was more laissez faire while Foster was more authoritarian—but they made a good team. While neither had a role in the project's design, both were genuinely enthusiastic about its concepts. Brennan was principal until 1978, when Foster took over.

Problems with the project initially were those of communication and acceptance; it was often unclear what the project was supposed to do. While faculty were aware of the project's goals, they did not completely accept them. It was difficult to bring about change in individual classrooms. Both new administrators had to build trust to overcome the previous principal's authoritarian, paper-oriented style.

The first project coordinator had a hard time accomplishing his responsibilities; in its fourth year the project was on its third coordinator. Brennan's time—80 to 90 percent of it—went to public relations for the project. Faculty picked pieces of the project that they could become enthusiastic about.

Dividing responsibility in the second year brought greater clarity about what was needed. New unit leaders were selected and received training in supervision techniques which helped them understand their responsibilities better. Some staff resistance, signalled by the common refrain, "Why don't you just let me teach?" continued.

The greatest needs early in the project were building faculty trust and cooperation. To do so, the new administrators had to counter the faculty's belief—based on their experience with the previous administration—that the principal did not value participatory decision-making. It was also necessary to find incentives for teachers to make long-term commitments to curriculum reform.

Both administration and faculty became more enthusiastic about the project as it developed; the keys seemed to be involvement and recognition. Instruction and supervision for unit leaders was offered during the summer, the school day was shortened twice a month to let the faculty plan, funds were made available to allow staff to visit other schools, and faculty received more recognition from the administrators.

Some covert staff resistance and sabotage continued, and Foster thought that his strong leadership style may have inhibited some teachers.

The View of the Staff.—Staff members generally began discussions of the project by referring to the need to improve the school's academic standards. A curriculum council of teachers and the vice-principal made major decisions about curriculum, allowing greater faculty involvement than is found in many schools.

The project coordinator oversaw operation of the project, spoke to the community and other groups about it, and conducted some inservice. The principal took the lead in project work such as negotiating budgets. Both were involved in inservice for other schools trying to implement the project.

The principal became more active when there was a conflict. More than previous principals, his style was one of fairly intensive interaction with faculty. While Foster was seen as more "autocratic" than previous principals, there was also the perception that he became that way only when it was appropriate to the situation. One teacher characterized his leadership as more "transactional" and less "by the book" than earlier principals.

Another teacher was not enthusiastic about the partici-

60

patory decision-making style, saying, "sometimes I think that participatory democracy is only there if you agree with the decision." While she often felt that participation slows decision-making, and sometimes wished that the principal would just make and announce a decision, she recognized that less faculty involvement would create more conflict.

Yet another teacher appreciated Foster's emphasis on increasing the school's academic standards and on involving faculty. He noted that the mature, aggressive staff was insistent about being involved. He applauded Foster's efforts to allow teachers to be observed by colleagues in the classroom, and to offer inservice classes on course goals. He thought that the principal had gained the trust of Watertown's faculty and that it was easy to take concerns and ideas to him. Characterizing the principal as "charismatic . . . dynamic, but low key . . . doesn't toot his own horn and is not at all an 'I' man but a 'we' man," this teacher particularly liked Foster's efforts to recognize outstanding contributions of faculty.

A fourth teacher rated Foster as "above average" in supporting innovations and as being theory based but always trying to make the application of theory to practice. He also raised two key points. First, what makes for a good principal depends on the location and whether there is a match between the principal's characterisitcs and the demands of community and school. Second, he believed that most faculty want strong leadership but also want to be involved in decisions, particularly ones about curriculum, so the principal must find the fine line between too much and too little direction.

FACILITATING BEHAVIORS

The View of the Principal.—Foster felt that the role of the principal was crucial to the success of a project, but emphasized that support must be more than verbal. He thought the principal should create a decision-making system that reflected support by involving teachers; he also felt the principal should provide resources, sit in on meetings, and help with problem-solving. Foster noted that statements of support that

61

are not backed by visible actions are soon perceived by teachers as mere lip-service. He also noted that "the project molds the principal," and that "some projects need a stronger principal than others." The presence of a project in the school will create new role expectations for the principal and will require the administrator to be very perceptive about how to implement the project.

Foster—like one of the teachers interviewed—identified the dilemma administrators face when they must both confront teachers and provide leadership to achieve goals, but also must have faculty participation in decisions.

The View of the Staff.—One project member interviewed saw the principal's role as one of getting resources to support the project, being flexible, being willing to take a risk, and recognizing project teachers while also rewarding "just the good hard-working teacher" who is not involved in the project. Another cited the principal's emphasis on curriculum and on getting teachers to examine their own behavior, his determination to involve teachers in decisions, and his activity in seeking public support for the magnet school.

RESTRAINING BEHAVIORS

The View of the Principal.—Foster mentioned two ways in which his behavior may have been unhelpful to the project. First, he felt the conflict between his role as administrator of the project and his role in the daily operations of the school. Often his involvement in the day-to-day operation of the school left little time for consideration of the long-range needs of the project. Second, he was initially hesitant in dealing with resistant teachers. Rather than trying to understand their feelings, he simply did not interact with them. He thought that one thing he learned from the project was the necessity of maintaining relationships with teachers who did not share his perspective.

The View of the Staff.—Staff members could identify few restraining behaviors on the part of the principal, citing instead such things as restrictive district policies, failure to meet some deadlines, and a waste of time on efforts that later seemed fairly unimportant.

INSERVICE TRAINING NEEDS

The View of the Principal.—Foster's experience was that a principal must take the initiative in seeking funds and opportunities for inservice. He did attend some district-sponsored inservice on general management skills, such as time management, did reading in management theory on his own, and attended workshops on conflict resolution and contract negotiations. He would like to see greater emphasis placed on inservice for administrators, including incentives for a systematic growth plan.

Foster also identified a need to develop "candid but tactful" evaluation systems, a way to identify deficiencies and support for correcting them. He would also like to develop an inservice plan jointly with the faculty to get feedback on his behavior. Finally, he would find benefit in visits to other schools to observe and talk with "master administrators" who had demonstrated strengths and skills.

The View of the Staff.—Teachers identified a variety of inservice needs for administrators. One thought that inservice could help the administrator learn and practice the participatory decision-making practices that were helpful in this project. He also thought principals needed help in organizing curriculum, since many come to the chief administrator's post from a vice-principalship in administration.

Another teacher thought that inservice should deal with change and how to promote it or live with it. One staff member thought that inservice might be a way to help overcome the insulation of teachers and administrators too commonly found, as well as helping "burned-out teachers and administrators."

Bringing teachers and administrators together seemed to be a common theme. As one teacher said, "I'm not sure you can separate administrator inservice from faculty inservice. Maybe

63

what you ought to do is offer inservice workshops for members of the community, the principal, and the teachers."

Also mentioned were problems of finding the appropriate time for inservice and the need to give teachers "hands on" experiences—perhaps by requiring that participants develop some product or project at the end of each inservice—as opposed to passive attendance at classroom presentations.

Inservice opportunities for administrators in this project were not separate from those offered to teachers. One valuable experience for the project director and principal was the inservice they designed and conducted for schools in another district to help them implement the project.

INTERPRETATIONS AND IMPLICATIONS

Interestingly, most people interviewed about the principal's role in this project quickly turned to his general leadership style and did not dwell on particular incidents or behaviors. Asked to describe facilitating or restraining behaviors, however, they did become fairly specific. They seemed to emphasize the differences between the present administration, which they liked, and previous ones, which they had not. Their long experience in this school had given most of them very definite views about their preferences.

For the individual attempting to implement change, the complexity of staff interaction and the firmness of individual views suggest that care would have to be taken in developing trust and communication, clarifying expectations and roles, and coming to agreement about critical issues such as faculty participation in decisions.

CASE SIX
Pierce: A Community Project

The case presented here is unusual for several reasons. The school is isolated, there has been a history of discontent and failure to support schools, and the project itself is aimed at serving the whole community.

The perceptions of interactions between the principal and project personnel are especially interesting when they are compared with the teachers' views of the principal. The conflict between expectations and obligations has had its effect on project operations, as it does in many sites. The implications for inservice education are particularly thought provoking as strategies for dealing with isolated and overburdened administrators.

THE COMMUNITY

Pierce School serves a community of approximately 5,000 persons. The town lacks many municipal services, such as sewers and police and fire protection. The only public park is the 11 acres surrounding the school.

Most people live in mobile home parks or in recently built small-tract homes; it is a transient community. Many residents have no children and many children have only one parent (or parent figure) at home. That means that the majority of the adult residents of the little district have neither reason nor opportunity to use the school and no inclination to support it.

Part of a district which had to close due to a lack of funds in the early seventies, Pierce is a new school. The land was purchased and the buildings constructed entirely on funds provided by a federal grant, one of only a very few that required no matching funds or financial backing from the local tax base.

The building contains large open classrooms and other classrooms designed specifically for community education. Most of the community education classrooms are used during the day either for regular classroom instruction or as special learning or resource centers.

The interior of the entire building is painted in off-white and light, airy colors, with many attractive displays throughout classrooms. It is functional without being sterile or cold, and the principal considers it to be the major accomplishment of the community education project.

65

The community education project had been operating for three years when we visited it. The two persons responsible for the project were George Hanna, the principal of Pierce, and Walter Ganeles, the district's community education coordinator. Several years ago, Ganeles was the district's public information officer and, in the wake of budget problems, was looking for a way to link the schools with their disaffected patrons. Hanna, then principal of another building, had already been working with the region's recreation department to develop an after-school program for his community and school. Though their perspectives differed, their goals were much the same, and Hanna and Ganeles have continued to work together for community education funding. Ganeles does the proposal writing. During the current year, the school's grant supports an on-site coordinator and an assistant coordinator. It would appear that the funding for next year may support only one site coordinator.

THE PRINCIPAL'S ROLE IN THE PROJECT

The principal in this project played a key role in its success. He had the respect of his teachers. Two teachers interviewed expressed a high degree of trust in his decisions. Also, he had been involved with the project since its inception. He worked with Ganeles to develop the initial proposal to fund it and the construction of the school. He went to bat with the board of education to maintain the project. He showed the teaching staff how the community education project could benefit them by providing released time for planning, by lowering the incidence of delinquency, and by increasing parental support. Teachers said that the program could not exist in this school without his support.

The View of the Principal.—Hanna noted that his role had changed considerably over the three years preceding the interview. He had helped write the initial proposal that led to the building of a primary and intermediate school. Before that, he was involved with obtaining community resources for an

66

after-school program for students. After the school was built and the community education program put in place, he continued to support the program, but he was not actively participating in it. He felt the community education coordinator should be responsible for the day-to-day operation of the project. He started to become more actively involved again as the project began to have greater impact on the community. For example, the frequent potlucks, movies, and other social events at the school called on him to be more active.

While the principal realized he must support the program if it were to flourish, he disagreed that he must be involved on a day-to-day basis. He felt that he could not give as much attention to the program as others would have liked. On the other hand, he saw that his support in front of the school board and community was very important.

The View of the Staff.—Some staff believed the principal should have been more involved with the program, but admitted he became more actively involved in the months just before our visit. Others thought that Hanna was adequately involved in the program. (The principal felt that the amount of involvement he had was appropriate, given the many other demands on his time.)

There was agreement on how the principal and others described his role in the project. Although there was some disagreement about what the principal *should* do in the project, there was not much difference in how the principal and others viewed what he had or had not done.

FACILITATING BEHAVIORS

The View of the Principal.—Hanna thought behaviors essential to the project included supporting the program with teachers, board, and community, for example, by mentioning the benefits of the program to teachers at staff meetings, going in front of the school board to support continuance of the program, and pointing out the benefits of the program to the public.

The View of the Staff.—Project members agreed that the be-

67

haviors Hanna cited were vital to the success of the program. They also believed that the principal should meet with the project staff frequently to listen to their needs and ideas about the project.

Also, the community education staff felt that the principal must be more actively involved if the project were to continue to be successful.

RESTRAINING BEHAVIORS

The View of the Principal.—Hanna recognized that the project staff believed he was too far removed from the project. His awareness was accompanied by his attempts to reduce the distance between himself and the staff.

The View of the Staff.—The community education staff agreed that the principal should assume more of a leadership role and day-to-day involvement with the project. In addition, they would like to have had more direct contact with the principal. They felt that they had to go through Ganeles to communicate with the principal. All three community education people interviewed felt that the principal had been more responsive in recent months.

As a group, project staff identified three kinds of restraining behaviors that could be harmful to a project: failing to assume and maintain an active leadership role, neglecting day-to-day involvement with project personnel and activities, and making communication occur through an intermediary.

INSERVICE TRAINING NEEDS

The principal and the staff were in fairly close agreement about facilitating behaviors that might be learned through inservice education. Both felt that workshops dealing with community education and ways to implement and evaluate these types of programs were useful. The staff would have liked to see the principal more trained in conducting meetings and group process skills. The principal wanted to have some hands-on experiences that he could immediately apply to his situation.

The major obstacles to inservice are time and location of inservice offerings rather than money, Hanna felt. There is not much in the way of inservice offerings for administrators within easy travel distance. Most inservice activities are conducted by the state administrators' association and are held in Portland or on the coast, and Hanna found it difficult to get away from the school for three or four days. He also commented that workshops he had attended were frequently not useful because they did not deal with his specific situation.

His recommendations for alternate forms of inservice included visiting model community education programs in other school districts, having a team of traveling inservice people who would spend several days on site assisting with specific problems, and holding more workshops in that geographical area. The traveling inservice team would need financial support from school districts around the state. It would also consist of people who could work on a variety of school problems and be innovative and responsive to local needs.

INTERPRETATIONS AND IMPLICATIONS

Pierce Intermediate School is probably not typical of most schools. It is in one of the fastest-growing communities in the state, one with no real history or tradition except, perhaps, alienation from the schools. Still, the case of Pierce does offer some insights into the principal's role in special projects, and raises several important issues.

The project staff repeatedly stated that the principal should take a more active role in the project by involving himself in day-to-day decisions, by showing more initiative (as by offering his own ideas rather than waiting to react to theirs), and by meeting more often with the community education staff. The principal, in contrast, felt that he continued to support the project but that major responsibility for it lay with the community education coordinator.

The conflict between the principal's style and the staff's expectations hits at one of the central dilemmas for principals, namely, "How much involvement in the project is appropriate, given all the other demands on a principal's time?" Do we have here a staff that is overly dependent on the principal's attention? We cannot perceive in this project major problems that appear to require the principal's intervention. How can this principal—and others in similar situations—walk the fine line between an intense involvement which takes considerable time and energy (and may decrease staff ownership in the project), on the one hand, and a too-distant relationship which staff interpret as lack of support, on the other?

The major implication for inservice training is more tailor-made training—specifically designed for the school and the needs identified by the principal and project staff. That would require bringing a team of inservice people to the site school, quickly identifying problems, and assisting the staff with their concerns.

CASE SEVEN
Harvesting a Volunteer Crop

This study deals with an externally initiated project run by volunteers at no cost to the school or district. As such, it has some distinctive characteristics of interest to the reader seeking ways to begin funded programs. Differentiating between those things that can happen when no financial strings and no traditional personnel policies encumber the project and things that can happen when accommodation must be made between district and agency policies and budgets helps to heighten awareness of some of the critical dynamics influencing the success of externally funded change projects.

THE COMMUNITY

Bordered on the east and west by mountains, Climax is surrounded on the valley floor by a number of small communities and is a center of commerce and transportation for the region. The county seat, it is also the site of a small community college.

A slowly increasing population has brought the number of residents up to more than 10,000, of whom about 35 percent are in the low-income category. Most minority groups are represented, but their numbers are very small.

The economy depends on timber and agriculture; a nationally known paper company is the area's largest single employer. Fewer than 9 percent of the residents are unemployed.

Old-time residents regard those who don't descend from original settlers as newcomers or tourists. The "newcomers" may have been in the community for fifity years, but they lack the clout of the founding families. The tourists are accorded little notice since it is clear they will stay for only a few years and then move on. Predictably, the most active community group is the newcomers.

Nearly 3,000 students attend the district's six elementary schools, the newly organized and innovatively designed middle school, and the senior high school. The town has a history of limited support for education. This is identified locally as the "conservative view" and is not representative of the younger professional community. Pupil-teacher ratios are high and the school board is hesitant to approve new programs.

Recently, the district became one of the first in Oregon to close its doors due to financial constraints. A revised budget was finally passed in mid-year. Budgets have fared considerably better since then, but the board remains cautious and conservative. Following the school closure, the chief administrator was eventually replaced by the present superintendent, almost 15 percent of the teachers were asked to leave the district or were discharged, policies were rewritten, and a management team was established. District goals were reformulated, roles and responsibilities clarified, and an operational philosphy established. The philosphy places responsibility for establishing educational goals with instructional staff and emphasizes board participation in decision-making. Once goals are established, commitment to their achievement is expected at all levels, though strategies for accomplishing objectives may vary among schools.

The success of this effort is evidenced by first-ballot ap-

71

proval of the last four operating levies. Morale in the district appears high. Teacher turnover is low and the management team is solidly established. The climate allows for innovation and, considering the conservative nature of the community, the district is quite progressive.

Crane School, in a middle to upper-middle income area, serves a comparatively large number of professional families, though a full range of socioeconomic levels is represented. Parents are supportive but reflect the community's conservative attitude toward education. Parents are involved in school programs and the PTA is active. There are very few minority children in the school, which serves just under 500 students in grades 1 through 6. The 30 staff members are experienced; morale and support of the administration are high. There is a good relationship between school and community and between staff and administration.

THE PROJECT

The project, one of six in this school, was a non-funded, locally developed, volunteer program that used community talent in support of the instructional program. Several factors interacted to provide an environment for the project. First, there was the norm of community involvement in the district: of the six elementary schools, five were active in their use of community volunteers. Second, there was a corresponding desire, especially among the young professional community, to participate in the school program. Principal Warren Redford had a strong orientation toward community involvement, and had academic and practical experience and training in using community resources. Finally, Crane was the site of a successful community school project which had recently been terminated due to budgetary constraints.

The primary objective of the project was to improve the instructional program by providing greater individual attention to pupils. A secondary objective was improved community relations. The project appeared successful in both respects, and much of its success was the product of the per-

72

sonalities and enthusiasm of the participants. The distinguishing features of the project were that the organization was essentially external to the school and that it was entirely volunteer. There was apparently no formal management structure, but rather an informal acceptance of appropriate responsibility.

The idea for a community involvement program was first proposed several years before our interview by the PTA president. The basic concept was a modification of a national PTA community involvement program. The PTA president also identified a person willing to coordinate the program. The principal was receptive to the idea and took the action necessary to gain district support. The PTA president and volunteer coordinator attended a workshop on community programs in another city; the volunteer coordinator then designed the program and developed the network of volunteers, and the community involvement project was initiated the following autumn.

THE PRINCIPAL'S ROLE IN THE PROJECT

In the initial stages of the project the principal's role was primarily that of facilitator. He probably exercised some informal influence but the design was, for the most part, created by the volunteer coordinator. The principal later became more actively involved, serving as liaison between the project and his staff, providing orientation and training to the community volunteers, and developing procedures and guidelines for operation of the project. Initial resistance to the project by some teachers was overcome by allowing staff participation to be voluntary. Community volunteers were used to the greatest degree at the primary level, mostly in support of the basic skills portion of the instructional program.

The principal of Crane School was a relatively young, active individual with nearly a decade of administrative experience. He appeared to have some administrative ambition beyond his position but was hesitant to leave the community.

73

Redford enjoyed the outdoor activities provided by the area and was very active in community affairs.

While the stimulus for the program was external to the school, the concept was not new to the principal, who previously had been involved in a community project in another state and had worked with a successful community school project at Crane School. He responded positively to the suggestion of the program and gave, according to the volunteer coordinator, "enthusiastic" support. Beyond serving as an advocate for the program, the principal skillfully influenced its design and focus. Parents were seeking involvement, but the principal was aware of the specific needs of the school and was able to shape the program to fit those needs. These were to reduce the child-adult ratio, to obtain increased clerical assistance, and to enhance the instructional program, specifically in the area of reading.

The principal gave direction to the program by his strong advocacy, orientation activities for volunteers, and informal awareness sessions for teachers. He attempted to maintain an atmosphere that allowed the program flexibility to meet the needs and desires of participants, yet also supported his own view of the purposes of a community involvement program.

In the implementation stage of the project the principal continued to be an advocate and facilitator, while leaving major responsibility for the project with the volunteer coordinator. The project had a very loose management structure; apparently management roles were never explicitly planned, but a good working arrangement evolved over time. It apparently fit the needs of the project and the expectations of the participants as well. The principal's main contribution to the project was his continuing support and enthusiasm, but he also developed systems for monitoring and evaluating the project.

FACILITATING BEHAVIORS

This project represented a fortunate match of needs, interests, and skill. The atmosphere created by the earlier community school program, the desire for involvement, the organizational skill of the volunteer coordinator, and the experience and training of the principal were all essential to success. Were a similar project to be developed in a setting without those conditions, it would seem that careful attention would need to be given to their development. The leadership of the principal would seem to require a combination of general skills in needs assessment, resource utilization, planning, and development, and project-specific skills having to do with organization and management. This implies two levels of inservice: first, the development of general skills appropriate to program-related administrative strategy; and second, the project-specific, site-specific knowledge and skill which are appropriate to a particular set of goals and objectives.

RESTRAINING BEHAVIORS

Perhaps because this project has been implemented so smoothly and effectively, persons we interviewed did not identify specific restraining behaviors of the principal.

INTERPRETATIONS AND IMPLICATIONS

The flexibility of the project meant that it could satisfy a diversity of needs and interests. For instance, the teacher interviewed thought that the project's greatest value was in providing support for the school's instructional program. The principal thought that the chief benefit was that it allowed the school to augment instructional programs, especially by giving more personal attention to individual students. The volunteer coordinator saw the major outcome as improved school-community relations. Each was able to identify an aspect of the project that fit his or her own frame of reference.

This case is noteworthy for principals who administer special projects—and for those who design inservice for administrators—in that the principal's role in this project was notably different from others in these case studies. In this instance, the principal did not take an active initiatory or leadership role; rather, he facilitated the efforts of others and

75

shaped the efforts of outside resources (the parents who volunteered) to meet the needs of the school. Also important is the fact that the project matched his earlier experiences and present enthusiasms. While some principals in these cases were in the position of needing to create the energy needed to make a project go, the principal of Crane was called on to harness and direct the energy that others already had.

How does a principal recognize when to step back and let others take the initiative? How can projects be made to satisfy the diverse needs and values of students and others in the school community? And how do principals recognize a project which can win their commitment even though it is someone else's idea? Those are among the issues raised in this case.

CASE EIGHT
Greenwood: A Mixed Bag

What happens to a project when the principal and staff have very different perceptions of the impact of administrative decisions and behavior? In this city school, staff and administration agreed upon desirable behaviors, but the staff did not see their principal as one who practiced what he preached. In describing inservice activities for project principals, the staff offered ideas that reflected their own discomfort with their administrator and attempted to provide ways of overcoming what they saw as his deficits. The principal's suggestions for inservice opportunities emphasized quite different topics. The reader may well ponder how these divergent views could be brought to greater congruence to enhance educational change.

THE COMMUNITY

Greenwood is a school in the southeastern corner of a small city; near the school, houses and lots are smaller than those in the more affluent suburbs. Taverns abound. The community has no major industry, but recently it has begun to acquire a reputation for its speciality shops. Young couples buying and remodeling older homes are bringing a greater socioeconomic diversity to the area.

Like its neighbors, Greenwood School is an old building, buff-colored, with pale trim outlining doors and windows. The inside of the school is dingy. The walls are bare of displays of children's work and are generally dirty. Graffiti covers the walls of the stairwells. The lockers are newly painted, but look nonetheless unkempt. The decay of the neighborhood seems to impinge on the atmosphere of the school.

Greenwood is a middle school, with grades 5 through 8. Its enrollment of fewer than 500 in September dropped below 400 by June. The community is stable, and many of the current students' parents went to Greenwood. Minorities comprise about one-fourth of the student body; some 16 percent—mainly Blacks—are bused in.

Four years before our study, Greenwood and a neighboring school merged, splitting the student populations into primary and middle school groups. Greenwood did not have a good reputation, but it was improving. The vandalism rate was the district's lowest, the school newspaper was said to be the best in the district, truancy and absenteeism were only minor problems, and Greenwood students were known for their good behavior on field trips.

Most of the staff of 31 teachers and nine aides were mature—they averaged more than ten years' experience and the median age was 45. A large turnover occurred a year prior to our study, as 18 of 26 teachers transferred.

THE PROJECT

The project at Greenwood School was "intended to develop, establish, and implement processes . . . to improve the delivery and impact of services to students identified as disruptive, emotionally handicapped, and/or learning disabled." The project employed a full-time coordinator, who was a social worker, two aides, and a secretary. In addition to direct services to students, the project provided training for regular faculty to back up project activities with students. The project, funded at $55,000, had completed its second developmental year at Greenwood and had been funded for one more year when we visited the school.

THE ROLE OF THE PRINCIPAL IN THE PROJECT

The View of the Principal.—Jim Flood, the principal, had served as chair of the city's special education committee, and the project was offered to him because of that interest. He saw the project as a way to serve the interests of the community and to meet valued goals for students. He accepted the project but expressed reservation, knowing from experience that special projects required staff development and personal involvement of the administration.

In the first year of the project, Flood recommended the development of staff readiness to accept and support the addition to school services. "A project has an effect on almost everybody in the school, from the custodian on," he said. Orientation sessions should clarify benefits to students and faculty. He maintained on-going interaction with the project director: "All aspects of the project must be shared."

As Flood described his involvement, he conveyed the impression of a college instructor addressing a class, diagramming the school's components on a flip chart. He had taught educational administration at a nearby college for several years, he explained, and had written textbooks and edited a professional educators' magazine. He spoke of the toll that federal projects take on an administrator and the need for appreciation of their payoff.

Administrators and teachers often differ in perceptions of the usefulness of a project, Flood said. Teachers sometimes fail to understand how a project will benefit them. They see the expenditure of money, the addition of another layer of administration, and a staff member with no class to supervise. The principal felt that this reaction could be overcome with open communication and active involvement of teachers in setting project objectives. Bulletins describing activities are not enough.

The faculty of Greenwood initially resisted the project, so

Flood held meetings to clarify project goals. This, he felt, was part of his role: "As principal, I am assigned to all projects to supervise." His past experience with federal projects had been extensive. He worked with other projects in the school, but the time he spent on them varied.

According to Flood, the role of a principal is very important for the success of a project. Whether he philosophically believes in its objectives is crucial. His whole mode of behavior, verbal and nonverbal, and the ways in which he works with the project can foster or hinder its development. The principal and the project director are equally responsible for the success of a project, he said.

What behaviors are most important? "Communication of project goals, developing incentives for teachers, and creating an environment that is conducive to success. Some principals don't give a damn and they leave everything to the project directors. Other principals wouldn't even allow a project in their school because it might affect the status quo. Having a project in your school does have its advantages and disadvantages. Any principal has to weight the costs. Is it really worth the extra effort that is going to be required when one compares the marginal return? Everything is time and energy and attitudes and priorities."

Flood felt that direct involvement of the principal was needed in the early stages of a project and also later "when there is a breakdown of support for the project." His administrative assistant attended meetings, because "you simply can't assume all responsibility—you must delegate."

The View of the Staff.—One staff member, Mary Marsh, reported that the principal had been very helpful initially, introducing her to the faculty and assigning her to a classroom ideally suited to the needs of the project. Unfortunately, this "ideal" classroom had been taken away from a popular teacher, and this move aroused dissension among the staff. The allocation of the room provided a focus for many differences in perception between Marsh and Flood. He had provided priority space for the project, and she appreciated that

79

and other examples of his thoughtfulness. Yet he did not ask the faculty how they felt about the project's location or acquire the cooperation of the teacher who was displaced. Marsh felt keenly the effects of this insensitivity, because the other faculty members took out on her and on the project their frustration about Flood's unilateral decision-making. Later Marsh shared in the faculty's frustration, because—possibly in light of the original resentment about the room—the principal changed the project to what Marsh called "a closet on the third floor." Again, no one was consulted about the decision, and her expression of dismay was greeted with a firm, "Sorry, but the decision has been made."

Marsh felt that the principal considered himself exceptionally competent, democratic, and communicative, but that, in fact, his help was frequently more trouble than it was worth. In the face of staff resistance, he mandated participation in the project. Marsh felt that Flood could have used his wide experience with special projects and academic affairs to explain the benefits of the project to the faculty. She thought he had never done this.

In the first year of the project, the principal was readily available for meetings and interactions with project staff. In the second year, he delegated responsibility to his administrative assistant. "Now I have trouble getting in to see him," said Marsh. "He is not accessible." In the first year she could counteract his arbitrariness with frequent consultations, but in the second year this method was unavailable to her. Her attempts to overcome faculty resistance by organizing a support services team to listen to teachers and encourage them to use project resources and by making the project's room and resources available to teachers were nullified by the lack of effective administrative support.

While Marsh cited several instances that indicated support from the principal (he co-signed letters, sent notes to teachers, and met with staff who seemed most resistant to the project), she also brought up several incidents suggestive of the principal's ambivalence or insensitivity to project needs. The most disappointing was his reassignment of the project to the third floor "closet." Then there was the slow withdrawal of the principal from meetings with the project director, his delegation of that involvement to his administrative assistant, and his becoming himself unavailable. This withdrawal was made worse by his dependence upon an ever-shrinking group of advisors. This led to her last criticism, that in the second year he made his decisions with no first-hand information about the project.

In general, Marsh thought that the principal was very supportive of the project activities and that his enthusiasm did not wane during implementation. She felt that his support was only rational, though, and that emotionally he still lived in a world where "these are naughty kids that we should discipline and expel." Marsh was sure that the principal would rate his support high, but she felt his help was not effective because he wasn't a very perceptive person. She felt he was naive in his methods of getting people involved.

Another staff member, John Lake, believed that Flood gave very little support to the project and was minimally involved. "In fact, I am not sure what he does." He observed that the administrative assistant and vice-principal worked with students more often then the principal did. He seemed to be out of the building a lot, serving on committees.

Lake agreed with Marsh that the faculty was resistant to the project in the beginning. He also agreed that Flood probably did not notice faculty resistance because he was poor at detecting things like that and did not have good interpersonal skills.

Lake thought that the greatest need of the project was for the principal to incorporate it into the total operation of the school and to provide avenues of communication and support. He mentioned that the placement of the project for next year was inappropriate and suggested a lack of support from the administration. Lake also wanted the principal to make a greater effort to find out why people did not support the project. Like Marsh, Lake identified instances which seemed

81

to indicate support by the principal (they were mostly the same ones Marsh cited), but offered still more examples that seemed to signal a lack of interest and support.

FACILITATING BEHAVIORS

The View of the Principal.—Asked to give examples of incidents that positively contributed to the project, Flood said, first, that the project got off to a "damn good start." A second factor was his close working relationship with the project staff. Third was the site environment: the community had considerable input. He could not think of any negative incidents.

The View of the Staff.—Marsh considered the principal's role very important in determining the success of the project. "It's crucial. You need . . . the principal to help incorporate the project director into the management team, to make the director part of a group. How the principal sets the project director up will be how the teacher perceives her, in all probability." Marsh thought principals spend too much time putting out fires and not enough time managing the affairs of the school. "I would want, if I were principal, to know about any project I have in my school."

The principal should be active in three areas of project implementation, according to Marsh. She believed the principal should be intellectually interested in the project and should make this interest evident in getting the project assigned to the school. The principal should become well acquainted with all aspects of the project; the project director should not have to fight tooth and nail for administrative involvement. Finally, she thought the principal should include project staff in general planning for school activities.

The administrative assistant believed that if the project is consistent with the larger needs of the community and the principal sees the benefit of the project, he will succeed. He must support the project visibly and verbally, however, if he is going to have it at all. He must front for it and get services and resources to provide for its growth and integrate it into the curriculum. The principal, the assistant believed, should

82

never let a project replace something that is there already; it should supplement the curriculum, not supplant an existing program. Inservice activities may bring about some change, but not in the basic philosophical orientation of the principal. Sometimes inservice can help a principal identify hidden agenda items.

RESTRAINING BEHAVIORS

The View of the Principal.—Flood believed that a principal cannot leave everything to project directors and expect success. Not caring and not wanting to interfere with the status quo are administrative attitudes deadly to special programs. Failure to communicate project goals, develop incentives for teachers, and create "an environment conducive to success" are behaviors Flood saw as damaging to innovative efforts.

The View of the Staff.—Lake noted that often principals don't listen; they flaunt their authority. Listening skills are regrettably lacking in administrators. He thought that principals were much better at dealing with parents and business details than with teachers.

Marsh viewed three kinds of behavior as limiting opportunities for project success: a principal's lack of awareness of territorial and symbolic aspects of school organization, a principal's absence from project meetings, and delegation of authority to a second-in-command.

INSERVICE TRAINING NEEDS

The View of the Principal.—Flood indicated that he had participated in many inservice activities and thought that most of them were excellent. He said he was aware of a continuing need for professional growth. He cautioned, though, against inservice activities offered during regular school time: it is important for the principal to "be among the troops." He said he would support inservice that has the incentive of a dinner or a stipend.

Flood thought attendance at national meetings was valuable, because they are often sources of new ideas. He attended

83

a national middle school conference and, as a result, initiated the pupil management specialist program in his school. He thought the process the school had developed for suspension of students was the best in the state. Traditional administration courses did not provide this stimulation for him. He suggested that inservice activities focus on managing time, prioritizing tasks, delegating responsibility, as well as communicating with staff. "Time," he said, "is money."

To arrange for inservice, "A principal can work through the ESD, look to the colleges, and participate in district-wide administrator inservice." Stress and communication skills had been high priority subjects for his district. Flood had recently taken a course in life-saving techniques which he considered much more important than three hours of reading methods. "Having a qualified person in the building might save a life."

The View of the Staff.—One staff member, considering administrators' inservice needs, made it clear that she thought the principal was as supportive as he knew how to be, but that he lacked the interpersonal skill needed to provide support without getting the project director in trouble with the faculty. She thought that effective inservice would cover communication skills, understanding of group processes, and understanding power and its effects. Another staff member also emphasized the importance of communication skills, so that project staff would feel free to express their opinions to the principal. Marsh also had several suggestions for inservice activities associated with implementing new projects in schools. Inservice could focus on solutions to problems commonly occurring with the placement of new projects in schools. First, she recommended working directly with school staff to prepare them to accept the project, to understand its goals, and to see how they support the general goals of the school. Second, she thinks principals should include the project director in the management team and encourage frequent and open communication between principal and director.

She also suggested that principals meet frequently with other principals and that superintendents invest more time in

84

overseeing principals' work. She thought it would be useful to have principals list long-range goals for each project; the principal and supervisor could then determine what kind of training would help achieve those goals.

Finally, she said that, since teachers and principals share an attitude of "who are you to tell me?" about inservice, it is important that the presenters of inservice activities establish credibility and trust.

INTERPRETATIONS AND IMPLICATIONS

A striking aspect of the information collected at Greenwood is the contrast between the broad agreement about necessary behaviors from a principal if a project is to be successful and the sharp differences between Flood and his staff as they interpreted and perceived his own behavior. The staff placed far more importance on the decision to shift the project room than did the principal; they also recognized that the original room assignment flew in the face of the faculty hierarchy. Whereas he considered his withdrawal from project activities a way to delegate authority and to increase staff ownership of the project, they saw it as evidence of a lack of interest in the operation. Since staff regard the principal's role in supporting the project enthusiastically as vital to project success, they seemed to resent his behavior and to feel frustrated by the distance that he created between himself and them.

It is interesting to wonder whether Flood, with his experience and pride in teaching administrative theory at the college level, was truly unaware of the value systems operating in his school. Was it a case of administrative overload? Was he, as staff believed, uninvolved and uncommitted to the project's goals and activities? Or were they simply too dependent upon the power of the principal to take the initiative and carry the effort themselves? And, if the latter is the case, what steps might the principal take to reduce such dependence, communicate his enthusiasm, and provide what all could agree was an acceptable level of public and material support?

85

Stress

When a small school is suddenly faced with a dramatically shifting population that funnels more students into than out of its system, stress increases for administrators and staff. The principal in this case was coping with such a population shift, trying to adjust programs and resources, facing a significant staff turnover, *and* attempting to support implementation of a comprehensive change project.

Dynamics of the setting may have heightened staff awareness of the principal's role in this project. We can see what they believe they need and what they expect from the administrator as they work at the innovation. The reader will find an unusually specific set of recommendations for principals' inservice education in this study.

THE COMMUNITY

The community comes as a surprise after the long, straight miles of driving through unpeopled pine woods. Where only a cafe and gas station once stood, a little cluster of roadside buildings has suddenly grown in the last few years into a noticeable settlement. Stores, restaurants, fast-food places, motels and homes—and homes and more homes—have slashed away the pines, creating almost overnight an unexpected, somewhat haphazard small town.

The town's greatest attractions seems to be its accessibility to some of the finest recreation areas in Oregon and a still-low cost of living. People crowd into numerous new developments of tract and mobile homes, though their jobs are usually elsewhere; the community is too new and small yet to offer much employment. Some people work in service jobs a half hour away in the county seat, some work in mills in other communities, and others in the woods. A fair number are on welfare or disability pensions.

A side road leads to the community's school, a collection of pre-fabs flanking an older large, wood-frame building. Growing pains are evident here. The school, which had fewer than 100 students five years ago, must now find room—and teachers—for nearly 600. New children stream in and often leave again in two or three months. In one recent month, for example, 20 students left while 50 others replaced them.

To house this expanding student body, the district administration, some miles away in the county seat, has used existing older structures and some modular classrooms. Communication and scheduling complications arising from such scattered facilities are a continuing challenge. Staffing provides 17 teachers for eight grades, and class loads inevitably run between 35 and 40 students per teacher.

The staff feels that they are "country cousins" to the modern town schools in the district, that they must shout louder and pound harder to be noticed. However, that is accepted as a fact of life and merely another problem to be dealt with.

THE PROJECT

Small rural schools usually have no staff to devote to applying for and supervising outside-funded projects. Frequently, when they identify an urgent need, they must meet it with a self-initiated, unfunded innovation. This was the case here.

The innovation was built around a new district-wide, individually paced reading program. Faced with as many as five reading skill levels in each overcrowded classroom, the staff had felt great frustration in trying to teach reading. The district's adoption, two years earlier, of a new coordinated reading series brought no change by itself to this classroom pressure, but did allow for a new approach within the school. The principal had seen it working in a town school a year earlier; he now felt it might help alleviate some of the pressures in his own school.

Fifteen sequential skill levels—spanning all grades—were covered in the reading series, allowing individual advancement at the student's own pace. This format enabled the staff to create cross-grade grouping so that students of comparable

87

skills could be in one room. It could not reduce the high student-teacher ratio, but could reduce the range of skills within each classroom. It required participation by the total staff, rescheduling to create one time slot for reading, and anticipation by the principal of materials needs.

The principal, Jeremy Watson, and his staff agreed on how the project was begun. (Only two of the teachers interviewed were at the school when the change was made.) The principal suggested cross-grade grouping as a possible way to manage pressures in the reading program. Staff members visited another school to observe the model system. The system was discussed in staff meetings and the staff as a whole decided to adapt it to their reading program. The need for one time slot for reading was identified by the group, which then agreed on the first period of the day; the principal then worked out the necessary rescheduling of classes. Teachers worked out other details of implementation; the principal ordered materials. Adjustments in the program were handled by the teachers, who also trained new staff members in the system.

THE PRINCIPAL'S ROLE IN THE PROJECT

All identified the importance of the principal as initiator and promoter of the idea, and as facilitator of the changes required for implementation.

As initiator, he brought the possibility of change to their attention; as promoter, he pointed out the advantages to students and to staff. The promotion, however, was shared; following the visit to observe the model, several teachers recognized the program's advantages and promoted the change among their fellow teachers.

The facilitator role was seen as exclusively the principal's, since he coordinated activities in the school and determined budget allocations. He also normally coordinated participation in outside-sponsored training opportunities.

FACILITATING BEHAVIORS

The visit to the model school arranged by Watson was the

key to staff understanding and acceptance of the change, since no real formal training was involved. An inservice conducted by the publisher of the reading series was considered by the staff "a complete bust" because it proved to be only another sales pitch offering no insights into the use of the program.

Assignment of levels among teachers was worked out by the teachers themselves according to personal preference and anticipated student loads. Estimates of needed materials were then made by teachers and given to the principal to be ordered. One teacher felt the excellence of the staff, as selected by the principal, contributed to the program's success.

RESTRAINING BEHAVIORS

When the program got under way, the principal seems to have turned to other concerns. This may be the point at which principal-staff interactions began to break down. All identified a role change by the principal since the program began, but what his role should have been appears to be an issue. Teachers and principal saw the program's functioning somewhat differently.

The View of the Principal.—The principal felt the teachers ran the program well without him. He stressed their "ownership" of it.

The View of the Staff.—While teachers generally reported satisfaction with the latitude the principal allowed them in carrying out the program, they strongly expressed a need for more awareness on his part of the program's mechanics, more assistance with day-to-day snags, more guidance and feedback (particularly to less-experienced teachers), and better anticipation of needs for materials as the distribution of students within the various levels fluctuated.

Some teachers wished more help with routine matters were available to the principal to free him to give the instructional leadership they would like. Others believed more effective organization of his tasks could accomplish the same end.

Whatever the reasons, teachers agreed that the principal spent too little time on the educational aspects of the school, including the reading program with its special demands, and too much on administrative and political demands which often took him away from the school altogether.

Individual responses to the principal's role varied. While the one set of generally negative reactions may have meant to imply blame of the principal, this was not stated openly, but was couched in such terms as, "You know, of course, that staff turnover this year is enormous. More than half are leaving." Several were leaving for reasons having nothing to do with the school itself, while at least two were leaving because they found the teaching conditions worse than they cared to cope with.

At the same time, those who expressed commitment to the community and intended to stay also expressed some reservations about the principal's managing of his role.

INSERVICE TRAINING NEEDS

All those interviewed felt the principal could benefit from well-planned inservice training beyond that presently available.

The View of the Principal.—Watson felt that the two aspects of inservice paramount in planning to meet principals' needs were content and format.

Content, he said, should respond to the needs of the particular principal working with a particular set of problems; the training that would be useful to each principal would vary according to his own situation and the extent of his or her background to deal with it. Time management, interpersonal communication skills, and questioning strategies were areas in which this principal felt the need for additional training.

Format is perhaps harder to think of imaginatively, since each person tends to think in terms of familiar processes. This principal remembered a week-long, statewide, intensive math training session as the most effective training he had received. The week allowed time to ingest a large body of information, with enough time off each day for the information to "simmer" before the next batch was added. The location allowed for concentration, free of the distractions of his job's constant demands. Having participants from all parts of the state allowed him to get to know other principals and to exchange views and experiences with them, which he believed is a real value in any training session. This calls for a group of at least 20 people, he thought, and time for interactions among participants. Other possible formats might include three-day to four-day workshops in different management skills, such as time management.

He would prefer two weeks at the end of June for attending several-day, intensive sessions, since this period is most free of other demands on school principals.

Useful training should involve both basic concepts and the skills application appropriate to those concepts, Watson said. While taking the training to the individual might allow for treatment of very specific concerns, it would also be likely to sacrifice opportunities to share with a larger, more diverse group. One kind of training in which on-site inservice might be most useful would involve the entire staff of a school in development of interpersonal communications skills.

The View of the Staff.—Most teachers interviewed said that useful training for the principal would include areas such as time management, organization, and communication skills—areas which he had also listed. Those who mentioned the last also indicated their own desire for similar training, although one stated emphatically that it should not include "group feelies—none of that touching stuff."

Teachers were generally unaware of present training opportunities for principals or of obstacles to that training. Those who had been acting principals had a clearer idea of the training that would be useful and of the demands with which a principal must be equipped to deal.

INTERPRETATIONS AND IMPLICATIONS

There were clearly some problems in this school, due in part to the rapidly growing student population which placed great strains on people and resources. Problems between the principal and his staff appeared to be due as much to inadequate communication as to other serious failures on either side. Beset by many pressures, the principal was thankful that his staff was capable of functioning independently; they in turn expressed the need for more attention and direction from him in their classroom activities.

None of these problems appeared to be specific to the innovation, nor would possible solutions be specific to that program alone. Training for the principal which might benefit the functioning of the program would also benefit other aspects of the school. However, the innovation functioned because the teachers themselves undertook the training of new staff members in a kind of informal inservice; assistance from the principal in that area would have been welcomed.

Lack of awareness seemed to be the key to the complaints expressed, both lack of awareness by the principal of the day-to-day functioning in classrooms, including the reading program and its particular needs, and lack of awareness by many of the staff of the range of concerns placing demands on the principal's time and energy.

The principal was central to many of the concerns expressed as coordinator of all activities and materials, as spokesman for the school to the district administration concerning assistance needed, and as leader of the people whose attitudes and perceptions guided the education of the students. The man in the role was liked personally by the most of the staff, but was considered lacking in some skills needed to facilitate the smooth operation of a school experiencing extreme pressures.

CASE TEN

Twilight of a Project

This case describes an unusually strong interaction among the factors critical to the support of an externally funded project. Economic pressures affected both school population and community support for the school; they also influenced the principal's behavior toward the project and turnover within faculty and administration.

The pervasive impact of the dying town on its school's attempts at innovation makes this narrative of special interest to those who seek educational change in depressed areas.

THE COMMUNITY

Fifteen years ago the Beacon Lumber Company began a gradual reduction in operation that culminated in 1978 with the shutdown of the Beacon mill. The mill closing was the dominant factor in the life of this small community; employment, city and school district revenues, and community stability have all been linked to the mill's fortunes.

The Beacon mill was the only major employer in this county, which was already among the poorest in the state. Without the mill, the town of Athens had to find a new economic base or face the prospect of continued decline. Agriculture has contributed to the economy, but it is not enough to provide adequate community support and services. Prospects of attracting new industry are dim. The community has investigated economic alternatives; one desirable option appears to be an attempt to capitalize on the increasing popularity of tourism in this part of the state. With outside capital the town may be able to generate a new economy. Its unique geographical and geological features and frontier-like environment could possibly stimulate enough interest to provide a major source of support. At the time of the interview, however, the outlook for the community and its school was not bright.

Over the past few years, district enrollment in elementary schools has dropped about 80 percent; in secondary, by about 50 percent. The enrollment projected for fall of 1979 was fewer than 150 students. The decline in enrollment has been matched by a decrease in financial support, as the district has lost the revenue generated by the Beacon mill and the other forest product industries. There appears to be a decline in community support for its schools and decreasing trust in

93

them, partly because of financial problems. As one result, there is low morale and instability among the school staff.

The superintendent (who is also the high school principal), in one of his first actions of his first year, sold the district-owned food service equipment and contracted with an outside agency to provide school lunches. The school board and community objected, the superintendent prevailed, and the tone for administration–school board relations was established. Later the board refused to accept the superintendent's recommendation to fire staff members he considered ineffective. Finally, after yet another confrontation with the board, the superintendent abruptly resigned. Also resigning during that year was the district's other administrator, the elementary school principal, who had been in that position only a few years. At the time of the interview, it was anticipated that at least half the district's teachers would resign by the beginning of the fall semester.

THE PROJECT

The proposal for a developmental reading project was written because student tests scores were showing significant drops in nearly every grade and subject area. It was a Title IV-C grant (we have no information on the project's goals or strategies) supporting a full-time project director and a half-time secretary. Its budget of some $40,000 per year was to be supplemented with gradually increasing funds from the district, but local funds were never made available.

The project was not generally viewed as having been institutionalized effectively and, in the view of most interviewed, was not likely to have lasting effects because of faculty transiency. Some materials and resources will remain in the schools, but there will be no funds or special personnel in the year following the interview.

The history and future of the project were deeply interwoven with the instability of the district. The proposal was written by an administrator who sought little assistance from teachers. The new elementary principal was hired without

94

knowledge of the project. A reading specialist employed as a project staff member found himself project director a few days later. The superintendent had little commitment to the project and was seen by the project director as varying between nonsupportive and negative.

The project was a low priority for the new elementary principal, Eric Horton; while he perceived himself as supportive, he was seen by faculty as being somewhat the opposite. This may have been an accurate perception or a reflection of a deeper discontent.

The project director initially believed that the project was reasonably straightforward and that it would be easily implemented. He soon became convinced, however, that the basic conception of the project was inappropriate and he proposed a new design. The funding agency approved the change, but left him with inservice commitments that were not especially appropriate to the revised project. The inservice program was conducted as planned, but follow-up was minimal and the impression left with participants was not favorable. One teacher, who perceived the district as having a history of not following through on programs, described this project as one more example of a well-established trend. Other teachers reported a general resistance toward the project among the staff.

The previous principal had been well liked by the faculty, and morale in the school was better than it had been in other years. When the project was awarded, the faculty was proud that such an honor had been bestowed upon their small district. When the principal unexpectedly left, the faculty was disappointed and disenchanted. These feelings may have moderated faculty enthusiasm toward both the project and the new project director.

The first project year was devoted mostly to planning and development of materials; some assistance was given to individual teachers. Little enthusiasm was generated for the project and it apparently functioned as an adjunct to the regular school program. The principal, who by the end of the first year understood the origin of the project, became less enthusiastic. The level of administrative and financial support from the district remained low during the first year. It was reported that the superintendent felt the project had been "dumped" on him by the departing principal; the situation was not improved when the superintendent abruptly quit.

The new superintendent offered no more support than his predecessor. The district still did not meet its financial commitment to the project, and the director reported having to "beg" for time to work with faculty, especially in the high school. All teachers were not required to participate; those who could have used the assistance the most sat on the sidelines. And so the project stumbled into its second year.

Despite little teacher enthusiasm and declining administrative support, the question of whether to continue or terminate the project had not been addressed during the entire first year. It did come up at the beginning of the second year, and that event may have been the single most important one in the life of the project.

During the first year Horton had experienced increasing frustration with the project. He became disenchanted with teachers who were not participating, and he was concerned about teacher behaviors that he believed indicated resistance or lack of interest. Teachers failed to follow directions of the project director and did not complete project activities on time, if at all. When he shared his observations and concerns with the director, the question of continuation was raised.

The project director responded by seeking and receiving support from teachers and community; although support was not overwhelming, a decision was reached to continue the project. For the first time, ownership of the project was acknowledged by someone other than the project director. The decision also gave the director an opportunity to elicit renewed support from the administration. Although this support continued to be more in word than in deed, it did result in greater effort to coordinate project activities with other programs and to facilitate delivery of resources, including staff time, for the project.

The project concluded with a workshop—a class for a credit—skillfully planned and conducted by the project director and well received by the faculty. It called for classroom application of a specific strategy, and teachers who partici-pated and made conscientious effort experienced considerable success. "John's Project," a title which reflects respect for the project director but which also gives some indication of the degree of ownership felt by the faculty, finally achieved some credibility and acceptance. As one teacher said, "I wish this workshop had come at the beginning rather than the end."

THE PRINCIPAL'S ROLE IN THE PROJECT

The View of the Principal.—Throughout the project the role of the principal, though reluctant, was central; to understand that role it is helpful to know something about him. Horton was a young, active individual who, after five years in another district as a successful elementary teacher, accepted his first administrative position as elementary principal in Athens. He described himself as having been a strongly motivated teacher who entered administration with hopes of sharing a humanis-tic view of education with a similarly motivated faculty. He was unable to characterize his own leadership style, but it can be described as one of facilitating and supporting achievement of commonly developed goals. He appeared to view the school faculty as a group bound together by common desires and mutual responsibility rather than as a collection of individuals. His comments suggested that the most critical features of any project are broad, cooperative participation in design and de-velopment and shared responsibility and commitment in im-plementation.

Horton described the principal's role as one of assuring staff participation, setting an attitudinal tone, being actively in-volved in working with staff and pupils, being responsible for communication and dissemination, and providing technical skills and assistance as needed. He cited the greatest need in

97

allowing the project to function in the school as the development of a "sense of ownership." Given this orientation, it is not difficult to imagine his response when he arrived to assume his first administrative position and found he had inherited a project, the author of which was absent, with a new director, an antagonistic superintendent, a staff which had not participated to any degree in designing it, and which nobody seemed to understand fully.

Even so, Horton described his initial reaction to the project as one of excitement and enthusiasm. There was a lack of clarity regarding expectations of his role and the nature of his involvement in the project, but he described his activities during the first year as being essentially the same as those of his faculty. He eventually identified his role as one of providing support and district resources and serving as a "sounding board" for the project director. Leadership, implementation, and operation of the project were considered the responsibility of the director. By his own admission, the principal's enthusiasm for the project waned over time and his involvement lessened. He perceived himself as continuing to give "superficial" support to the project and was a participant in the final workshop.

The View of the Staff.—The faculty's assessment of the principal's role varied from neutral to negative. Most assumed that he had known about the project before he arrived. One believed the principal's initial reaction to be favorable and another reportt that he "did take part in the workshop and seemed interested." The teachers themselves, while pleased to have been awarded the funding, were not overly excited and had little understanding of the project. Most agreed that the principal was less than enthusiastic and saw him as providing little, if any, support to the project.

The project director perceived the role of the principal differently from the faculty. He agreed that the principal was not strongly committed to the project but did feel some support for it and for himself personally. He felt this support increased, mostly through his own initiative, as the project neared its conclusion.

FACILITATING BEHAVIORS

The View of the Principal.—The principal described his ideal role as assuring participation, demonstrating values, setting tone, actively involving others, and facilitating communication and technical assistance. Neither the principal nor the teachers were able to define his leadership style. Adjectives they used included "variable, informal, not authoritative, not direct, laissez-faire, apathetic, relaxed, humanistic."

The View of the Staff.—The desirable behaviors expressed by teachers and principal were similar. Teachers expected the principal to be an active participant, to be knowledgeable about the project, to be supportive, and to clarify roles and expectations. The project director said it would have been helpful if administrators had communicated their support to teachers and believed that the principal could have contributed more by understanding the project more fully, coordinating it more carefully with other school activities, and in general lending more credibility to the project through aggressive leadership and support. The project director was leaving the school district upon completion of the grant.

RESTRAINING BEHAVIORS

The View of the Principal.—At the bottom of the dissatisfaction between principal and staff appreared to lie a basic philosophical difference which was perhaps brought to the fore by the project. The principal saw a need for a supportive behavior, but he viewed himself as a facilitator, not a director.

The View of the Staff.—Teachers were generally critical of the principal's role. They understood that the project director had been given responsibility for management of the project, but they believed that administrative leadership and demonstrations of interest and support were critical missing elements. Administrative requirements were seen as competing with project needs, lack of verbal support was interpreted as

99

disapproval, and failure to assume leadership was cited as a primary cause of the low level of teacher enthusiasm. There was general agreement that, had the principal been more involved, the project would have enjoyed greater success.

The faculty clearly wanted to respond to external motivation and direction; they were looking for strong leadership and reinforcement, as can be seen in these paraphrased comments:

- A lot of staff weren't sure of its importance and saw the project as a waste of time. The principal encouraged staff resistance.
- The principal should have convinced teachers that the project was valuable.
- Time should have been given to work on the project. Teachers were asked to take their own time to attend the required class.
- Teachers would have been motivated more if they had received more direction from an administrator or a person with some power in the system.
- The principal did not attend meetings and acted bored or left early when he was present. He never asked teachers about what they were doing.
- If the principal had given direction, teachers would have been more responsive.
- It's mandatory to have someone in control. The principal must give total support or the project doesn't have much chance of success.
- The principal should follow the progress of the project through regular contact with teachers, informal assessment, and reinforcement.

INSERVICE TRAINING NEEDS

Assessing inservice training needs in this project is a little like asking, "Can this marriage be saved?" History and environment may have influenced the project so strongly that anything less than a total rearrangement of forces and constraints would have had little effect. Yet the project did enjoy some limited success and that success might have been greater had the roles of the primary participants developed somewhat differently.

Inservice needs suggested by the participants fell into three categories. First, the principal should have had an intimate knowledge of the project. He should have understood guidelines, mandates, role expectations, budget, activities, desired outcomes, etc. He should have known the project well enough to communicate purpose and goals effectively, to orient and motivate teachers, and to offer leadership in project implementation. Second, the principal should have had a repertoire of skills in change strategies, program implementation, organizational planning and development, and administrative leadership in project management. A third category of need was training in motivational and interpersonal skill. Of the three categories, the most often and most emphatically mentioned was knowledge of the project.

INTERPRETATIONS AND IMPLICATIONS

Two related themes regarding the role of the principal emerge repeatedly. First the principal is the leader of the school and his or her advocacy is critical to the success of its programs. Second, the principal must have knowledge and commitment that are demonstrated through participation. There was agreement that the most critical inservice needs were project specific. The principal must understand the purpose, requirements, outcomes, etc. of a project before effective leadership can be exerted.

If this project were a western movie, the project director would probably be shown riding away on a white horse while the principal departed via the back streets. Neither perception is accurate. It is not possible to separate the history of this project from the history of the district and the community, and perhaps the most basic mistake was in applying for the grant in the first place. Some teachers who will remain are optimistic that the impact of the project will continue, but the Athens schools will open next year with a new administration, an essentially new faculty, significantly reduced enrollment,

101

quite possibly without a budget, and continuing problems of financing and community support. It is more likely that the Athens reading project will become yet another episode in the history of a struggling school district.

I Never Did See the Principal

The circumstances described in this case are an unusually potent mixture of factors leading to the failure of the school's project. The problems of leadership, ownership, administrative support, and resource allocation that afflicted this project include many characteristics identified in other cases as restraining behaviors. More than a year after the demise of the project, people in the school and district were able to cite specific difficulties they'd encountered.

A question arises from this study: What can a principal do to ensure that project staff do not view delegation of authority as neglect or lack of interest?

THE COMMUNITY

This is a river city, and its rich farmland attracted many settlers with the promise of abundant harvests and easy transportation. On its edges one can still see orchards, row crops, and cattle. There are no slums or ghettos here, but there are poorly tended neighborhoods along the tracks and near the warehouses and plants. One notices, however, that people everywhere grow things and that most residences have trees and shrubs outside and potted plants in windows. In the more prosperous areas, lawns and gardens are meticulously cared for. There are few stone or brick houses; most are wood and a few are Victorian.

Over the years local artists and craftspeople have tried to set up galleries and shops. Except for one long-established showplace run by an artists' association, most succumb to the apathy of area clientele. The standard department stores, discount stores, and fast-food chains, dreary in their sameness

102

across the country, are patronized by most of the residents.

There is about this city a feeling it has no clear identity, both because it so resembles many other small American cities and because it hasn't completely outgrown its earlier agricultural self.

The school district, which serves about 26,000 students, copes with several unusual influences. In the city or nearby are three institutions of higher learning (each with programs preparing students for occupations in education), an educational development institution, and a particularly powerful county educational district. So the city's schools are in high demand as research and testing sites, the county office has some control over the district's finances and policies, and teachers' enrollments are prized by the colleges as a way to offset declining undergraduate enrollment.

THE PROJECT

For most people, there's not much excitement in exploring the reasons an enterprise failed. So it would not have been surprising if the principal had met the request to study the project with a firm rejection. Instead, he went to some trouble to construct a list of people who'd been involved in the project and to assign the vice-principal the task of making interview arrangements.

The innovation in this high school (and in the adjoining junior high) was one to promote visual literacy by using non-print media as teaching materials. The project had been developed in another district where a particularly enthusiastic teacher had prepared the curriculum and materials. It was brought to this city by a district specialist who wanted to promote that kind of learning as an extension of library instruction and as a way to help students expand their access to information. None of the school people interviewed knew how the program got to the high school; it wasn't until the researcher talked with the specialist that the process was identified.

Following the decision to try the project, several activities

103

were planned to introduce its concepts and materials to teachers. A first step was a presentation by the program's originator. No one recalls who went to the presentation or how people were chosen to go. Nor do people remember clearly who selected the administrators and teachers who made two trips to the originating district to see how materials were used and to talk with students and teachers. At some point, another administrative decision was made, this time by the principal, who selected those who were to be directly involved in the project. Those people were to attend a summer workshop, for which they would be paid, to receive training in the project. Again, it is unclear how those selections were made, and conflicting reports of these events are given by those who were interviewed.

The program's originator had contracted with the school district to spend time at the site school during implementation to provide instruction, answer questions, and generally serve as a support for teachers. One interviewee said that she was to have visited every two weeks, but came every six instead. Whatever the actual agreement and performance, site personnel consistently reported that they saw less of the originator than they had hoped or believed they would. Interestingly, though, they seemed uniformly appreciative of her talents and enthusiasm. They believed she had overextended herself and just didn't have time to do all the things expected of her. One less approving comment was that materials were often late in arriving and were unclear.

It quickly became apparent that those whom the principal had identified as being in the project were not at all clear about who was directing it. When asked who was responsible for leadership and organization, various people mentioned the originator of the materials, the district media specialist, the vice-principal, and the head librarian. No consensus existed about whose baby it was.

In the fall of the implementation year, a first-year teacher was assigned to teach one of the courses associated with the project. For several reasons, that assignment seemed to be unfortunate: the teacher was inexperienced and had not requested the course, and the department in which the course was taught was not strongly supportive of the project and did not provide much assistance to the teacher. For a number of reasons (some unassociated with the project) the new teacher left at mid-year and was replaced by an experienced teacher who did not place much value on the project or continuing the course.

It appears that about six people were identified with the project, though none was "in charge" of the operation. There was a real attempt to diffuse the materials through various disciplines, but what actually happened was that the teachers who were *already* using a variety of instructional media embraced the concepts of the project. There is no evidence that any converts were made. Several people, reflecting upon the project's isolation from on-going school practices, thought that it was inevitable that ideas won't cross departments. There also was a strong feeling that people did not want to "steal" or use others' ideas intact.

The project actually existed for only half a year, although one person interviewed (more than a year later) believed that the project was still functioning because *she* was still using some of the materials and concepts.

THE PRINCIPAL'S ROLE IN THE PROJECT

The View of the Vice-Principal.—Each effort the researcher made to contact the building principal was unsuccessful. Arrangments for the study had been made by the vice-principal and it seemed that—once that task had been delegated—all queries were also to be handled by the vice-principal. As he reviewed the project's history and problems, he cited these factors as important:

• When the project was instituted, there was a district-wide mandate for change in numerous curricular areas. This particular project was considered less important than some others, and not much attention was focused on it.

105

- Although others had called the project a model program, the vice-principal believed that it was an optional activity that could be dropped.
- In high schools in general, there is a territorial problem of trying to move methods and ideas across departments.
- The project wasn't a high priority to the teachers; they'd been through across-the-board pushes for rapid and broad changes in the past three years.
- There was some resistance to the project as something that had come from the outside. Bringing in someone else's ideas carried the implication that what the faculty were doing was wrong. There also was some feeling that the school had become an expeditor for someone else's creation.
- At least one key faculty member believed that what the project was supposed to accomplish had already been done; it was a duplication.

The vice-principal's attitude toward the project was reflected in a decision he made when the first-year teacher, who had been assigned the demonstration course, was replaced. The experienced teacher who followed said that he couldn't use the program, and the vice-principal agreed that he didn't have to continue it.

He believed he had been very enthusiastic about the visit to the originating school site, that he had helped select the people to participate in the project, and that he had hoped it would make real progress. He checked on how people felt once the project was under way but he didn't push it.

The View of the Staff.—As best events can be reconstructed, it appears that the principal had some early involvement through a committee on media needs; he seemed to drop out when the new program was transported from the original site. The vice-principal, who was new to the school, took over then and adopted the principal's leadership style. That style was consistently described as laissez faire: if a teacher wants to try out something, he or she is encouraged to go ahead and do it.

People added that the vice-principal generally stayed out of their way, letting them do their own thing. He did not seem to be withholding support, but neither did he involve himself overtly in such efforts after he had given his approval.

The project director wanted to "sell" teachers on the concept of the library as a media center; rather than re-invent the wheel, he found the other district's existing program an ideal vehicle, so he arranged to transport it into his own district.

The specialist viewed both principal and vice-principal as willing but terribly harassed by many other pressures and tasks. He thought they did almost nothing to support the project, and generally had little interest in or understanding of curriculum. He felt they were supportive, and gave time and teachers to the project, but they were just not able to assist effectively.

Because the faculty seemed to like the laissez-faire leadership style of the principal and the vice-principal, they did not consider the absence of active support for the project to be an administrative fault. Only one person expressed dissatisfaction with the absence of leadership, and he identified the major reason for the lack of support as a lack of understanding of media. That meant, he thought, that the administrators were unable to place sufficient value on the project to publicize it properly and to enlist faculty support.

FACILITATING BEHAVIORS

The View of the Vice-Principal.—To make a project successful, the vice-principal noted, the administrator must be a prime source of support. He or she gives the cue to teachers and must be supportive and enthusiastic. Critical times for displaying support and enthusiasm are at the outset, when both time and money must be invested, and during evaluations and checkpoints during the project's life.

The View of the Staff.—Recommendations the specialist made about what administrators should do to help an innovation included: publicly stating to the faculty his or her support of the project, feeling and showing enthusiasm for the effort, understanding the educational values of the project, asking teachers how things are going, and being a knowledgeable and close support. This last behavior was emphasized as the one most important to a project's success.

RESTRAINING BEHAVIORS

The View of the Vice-Principal.—The vice-principal suggested some circumstances that hindered implementation of the project, but none involved the behavior of the principal. It is possible to infer, however, that the believed chances for success would be severely restricted if the principal did not act as a prime source of support, was not visibly enthusiastic about the undertaking, and did not invest time, money, and attention in the project.

The View of the Staff.—Staff members usually began thinking about principals' unhelpful behaviors by considering unattended needs in their own project. Among the areas in which they thought assistance and support were lacking were:

- appropriate space for the project, including classrooms;
- assignment of a staff of sufficient size to demonstrate commitment to the project by the administration and also to assist teachers;
- bringing achieving students into the program early so the project is not viewed as only something for those who fail in school;
- assigning experienced teachers to the project's courses and letting them choose the assignment rather than imposing it on them;
- inservice planning time to work through units, materials, etc.;
- educating faculty, parents, and students about the legitimacy of the project's goals;
- active support of the administrators and key faculty;
- an enthusiastic teacher to invest time and interest in the project.

The district specialist described his concerns about the project. Of those, the ones most directly related to the princi-

108

pal's role were: teachers involved did not have a thorough understanding of concepts and materials; one needs to provide time to talk through the problems that are inevitable in any innovation (there seemed to be no regularly scheduled meetings of project participants); and there were problems of jealousy, encroachment on others' time and students.

INSERVICE TRAINING NEEDS

Most people interviewed throught that at least one of the administrators (preferably the principal) should have taken the workshop training and tried out project materials. They thought the principal would have been a stronger advocate if he had more knowledge of the project. Oddly, though, that observation was usually accompanied by a kind of disclaimer: well, he has a lot of other things to do; he treats all special programs the same way and it is to teachers' credit if they're successful; and that's fair of him, etc.

Beyond that, people in the school had little to offer by way of suggestions about inservice.

INTERPRETATIONS AND IMPLICATIONS

The striking thing about this case is the discrepancy between what we have called "espoused theory" and "theory-in-practice." All people interviewed identified public and continuing administrative support as vital to the success of a project, but support was conspicuously absent in this project. Only one person, however, seemed to recognize the gap between what people said was important and how both administration and faculty were behaving. On the one hand, people said support was important, but on the other hand no one seemed to connect the demise of the project with the lack of support given it by both faculty and administration. Indeed, most people expressed a preference for the hands-off, abdicating style of the principal.

A second striking aspect of the case was the lack of clear leadership. "They" made decisions, but "they" had no real identity to anyone other than the district specialist. No provision, apparently, was made to form a team within the school to manage the project's operations or to integrate the role of the district specialist with those who were to carry out "his" innovation.

The project had so little identity within the school that one teacher thought it was still operating a year after it died. That suggests that contacts among project faculty were neither regular nor informative. Also, several persons interviewed declared far stronger allegiances to their academic departments than to the concepts promoted by the innovation; when conflict arose, they chose the department rather than the project.

Our overall impression is that the project had virtually no impact on the way teachers used media. Some teachers used the materials when they were compatible with present practice, but teachers not involved in the project simply continued as before.

It is not clear what would be a remedy for the central problem in this project: neither principal nor staff seemed to have enough commitment or energy for the change to make it work. This school probably illustrates what happens when the minimum conditions of readiness are simply not in place before the change is initiated. As Belle Kaufmann would say, "Let it be a challenge to you!" And so the project fell down the staircase.

CHAPTER 3

Findings of the Study

In this chapter we describe the patterns of success and failure we found in the cases presented in Chapter 2 and what principals did to contribute to the fate of the change. First we review key points about the projects and the principals' roles. We then describe the four stages we found in the life cycles of projects and how principals' behaviors were adapted to each stage. Following that is a presentation of the eight critical behaviors of principals that shaped success or failure.

Characteristics of the Cases

The eleven cases described in Chapter 2 represent a variety of settings, funding sources, topics, kinds of schools, scopes of application, actions of the principal, and degrees of success. In general, there was no consistent pattern in these characteristics—secondary schools were not notably more successful than elementary ones, some reading projects succeeded while others failed, and so on. Success or failure did not depend on these characteristics alone; rather, a project's outcome depended on the interplay of several forces, especially the role of the principal.

Here in brief are the essential characteristics of the cases as a group:

- Six schools were elementary, while five were secondary.

111

- Three projects were about reading, four about curriculum changes, and the remaining four about special education or other topics.
- Two schools were in urban settings, four were in suburbs or small towns, and five were in rural areas.
- Seven projects were funded by federal sources, and others used money from a variety of sources.
- Principals varied in age and experience; some were in their first principalship while others had 30 years of experience. Experienced principals were slightly more successful than beginning ones, but that pattern is not strong; what the principal *does* apparently counts more than what she or he *is*.
- Projects ranged in scope from a summer "add-on" to extensive curricular and organizational change. Some projects added staff for the project while others used existing faculty. Some required the involvement of teachers but others were voluntary.
- Impetus for the project varied: one re-created a prior success, one grew out of a comprehensive needs assessment, and in other cases a project which seemed to match already felt needs was made available to the school.
- In seven projects the initiative came from the principal but in others it came from a variety of sources—the PTA president, faculty members, or other district personnel.

No single characteristic (or combination of characteristics) guaranteed success to a project. We were apparently successful in selecting a diverse sample of schools. With that in mind, we now turn to the characteristics we intended to isolate—the role of the principal.

The Principal's Many Tasks

Here, in capsule form, are the principals' and others' descriptions of what each principal did in his or her project.

112

Joe Lyons was the prime mover in identifying the need for a project and in finding the solution: he located a funding source and wrote the proposal. In many formal and informal meetings of staff and parents, he created awareness of the need and recognition of the problem. There was clear delegation to the staff, but it was backed by substantial, continuing support. He was the project's public relations man, worked with central office people to expedite things, and was "bus driver and tour guide." At the end he tied up loose ends, edited the final product, and hosted a social event to toast the project's success.

Key: Lyons successfully made the transition from leader to manager. At first exercising considerable initiative in creating awareness and providing a solution, he then turned the project over to a capable staff but continued to demonstrate support and helpfulness.

CASE 2: MOVING BACKSTAGE

Dissatisfied with the school's career education program, Paul Harrison made repeated efforts to gain faculty acceptance before succeeding with a strategy that worked with individual departments and recognized teachers' expertise. He took care of logistics and prepared materials. After giving clear delegation to the staff, he kept attention focused on clear goals and roles, and encouraged teacher leadership. Keeping himself informed of progress throughout the project, he continued to provide administrative support.

Key: Harrison, like Lyons, made the successful transition from an initiating and leadership role to a more managerial and facilitating one.

CASE 3: INSIGHT AND SKILLS

Identifying a problem in students' test scores, Martin Lawrence held several "low-key awareness sessions" with parents and faculty. When people committed themselves to launching the project, he turned to dealing with the funding agency and central office. After hiring competent project staff, he delegated responsibility to them while he provided support, resources, and liaison for the project.

Key: Lawrence also began as a leader and then shifted at an appropriate time into the role of manager. Much of his help consisted of linking the project with important parts of the system.

CASE 4: SUCCESS IN A VERY SMALL SCHOOL

A happy combination of the widespread recognition of the problem and the availability of a project that fit the head teacher's philosophy allowed Pamela Bishop to involve her small staff immediately in deciding to adopt the project. She was the "buffer" who protected the project from criticism, while she also gave the staff verbal support, clear goals, and latitude to operate.

Key: The staff credited Bishop with creating a school climate receptive to the project, one that encouraged staff initiative. Given the early staff involvement, she did not have to supply the driving energy for the project and her role was mainly a facilitating one.

CASE 5: WATERTOWN

Bill Foster enthusiastically supported the project even though he did not come to the school until after it had begun. (He also seems to have been a welcome change from some prior administrators.) His leadership consisted mainly of aggressively involving the staff in decision-making and in making his commitment clear through specific supportive actions, while allowing the project director and teacher leaders to function effectively.

Key: Foster recognized that the mature staff was eager for involvement in decision-making, a desire that was compatible with his philosophy and style. He was active in securing resources for the project, in recognizing the contributions of teachers, and in keeping attention focused on issues of curriculum and academic standards.

CASE 6: A COMMUNITY PROJECT

George Hanna followed the familiar pattern of providing the initiative at first and then stepping back into a more managerial role, but in this case it was not working well. He brought the project into the school and continued to provide verbal support, public relations, and linking functions, but the staff complained that it was hard to get access to him and that he did not provide enough direction.

Key: The staff wanted a leader and director, but the principal was more comfortable as a helper and facilitator, so there was an imbalance between the principal's style and the staff's expectations.

CASE 7: HARVESTING A VOLUNTEER CROP

This case was unusual in that principal Warren Redford did not need to provide the driving energy, since it was coming from the PTA president and community volunteers. He helped create staff awareness of the project and directed the outside energy to meet the particular needs of the school. Making teachers' participation voluntary helped allay their fears. He was an advocate for the project and created monitoring and evaluation systems for it.

Key: Redford's low-key facilitator style was appropriate to this situation. Overcrowded classrooms created a clear and felt need, while the solution lay in the community, so the principal functioned mainly as a helper.

CASE 8: A MIXED BAG

At first glance, Jim Flood seemed to do all the right things. He solicited staff support, provided space, and followed the pattern of "first a leader, then a manager." Yet all was not well with this project. He brought in the project despite faculty resistance, upset the staff by taking away a teacher's room (without notice) for the project, and gave what the staff considered very mixed signals. Some actions seemed to speak of support while others were read as showing a lack of interest or competence.

115

Key: The striking thing about this case is the many discrepancies—between the principal's words and the staff's view of his actions, between the conflicting sets of signals he seemed to give them, and so on. Perhaps the discrepancies themselves, the lack of clarity between staff and principal, are the key to understanding this floundering project.

CASE 9: STRESS

Here, principal Jeremy Watson took the initiative to secure the reading project, though the staff participated in the decision to adopt it. While he continued to provide logistical support, his delegation of responsibility to the staff was interpreted as a withdrawal due to lessened interest. He encouraged teacher ownership of the project while they complained of a lack of leadership and felt that administrivia diverted him from attending to the school's instructional program.

Key: While Watson was well liked as a person, he was not seen as an effective manager—neither well organized nor sufficiently directive. Like some other cases, this project seemed to suffer from a lack of clarity and agreement between principal and staff about his role.

CASE 10: TWILIGHT OF A PROJECT

Principal Eric Horton inherited this project in a high-conflict situation. He had little understanding of the project or enthusiasm for it, and by all accounts seemed to give the project superficial support and little attention.

Key: A failure to confront the issue of continuing the project is probably the key here (if, indeed, the project should have been attempted at all). Neither the staff nor the principal seemed to have much energy for the project, and the principal's desire to be a low-key facilitator was not well matched to the staff's desire for more leadership and indications of interest in the project.

CASE 11: I NEVER DID SEE THE PRINCIPAL

Apparently the staff never saw the principal either. He

made the decision to adopt the project but then turned every-thing over to the assistant principal . . . or maybe the librarian was in charge . . . or the project director . . . was anybody in charge? With almost complete lack of clarity about the project, energy to make it go, commitment to its activities, and under-standing of who was in charge, this project was virtually˘ stillborn.

Key: While the laissez-faire style of both principal and as-sistant principal admirably matched the staff's desire to be left alone, that combination does not provide the energy needed to initiate and maintain a project. Nobody seemed to want the project very much, and it died from the neglect of both princi-pal and staff.

These short descriptions of the principal's role give us sev-eral clues to successful project management.

First, somebody has to have energy for the project—recognizing the existence of a problem, feeling committed to finding a solution, and expending the effort needed to make it work. That happened in two ways in successful projects. In some cases the principal supplied the energy. He or she sensed the need but quickly involved staff and others in recognizing and "owning" the problem and ways to solve it. These princi-pals began as leaders who took the initiative but then moved backstage into managerial roles in which they supplied sup-port and resources to the people doing the central tasks of the project. In other cases, the energy was supplied by others and the main role of the principal was one of channelling, direct-ing, and supporting that effort. Failure occurred when that energy was lacking. If the principal played *only* a facilitating role when there was not other energy to drive the project, it muddled along as in Case 9. When the principal supplied the initiative but then withdrew, as in Case 8, the project floun-dered. When neither the principal nor the staff gave any en-ergy to the project, it was stillborn, as in Case 11.

Second, effective management of the projects depended on a good match between the principal's style and the staff's expectations. (We will have much to say about this aspect later in this chapter.) Projects were in trouble when there was a decided imbalance in style and expectation. However, there was also trouble when the match, in Case 11, did not supply any energy for the project.[1]

Finally, we see that principals performed a variety of roles and that these roles changed during the life of the project. The successful principal, in composite, was many things: he or she was a *believer*, feeling a genuine commitment to the project; an *advocate* who promoted and defended the project before a variety of audiences; a *linker* who connected the project with other parts of the system; a *resource acquirer* who obtained and allocated tangible and intangible resources for the project; an *employer* who hired project staff or assigned teachers to it; a *leader* who supplied initiative, energy, and direction; a *manager* who provided problem-solving assistance and support; a *delegator* who "moved backstage" when teachers assumed leadership; a *supporter* with words of encouragement and acts of assistance; and an *information source* who gave feedback to teachers and project staff.

About Leadership Style

A variety of styles seemed to lead to success, and the particular style used apparently mattered less than did the match between the person, the group, the task, and the situation.

Here are descriptions of the principals' styles as they and others reported them to us. The teachers' reports, of course, tell us as much about what they want from the principal as they do about what the principal actually did.

We use the categories of Tannenbaum and Schmidt (1973) to characterize the principals' styles. We will have more to say about the styles in the next chapter, but here is a brief de-

---

[1] We do not have information on some kinds of principals. For instance, we have no case in which the principal was overactive, keeping all responsibility to himself or herself. We also have no case in which the principal declared open hostility toward the project. But then, neither of those styles would seem to teach us much about successful project management.

scription of what they mean. They can be put in the form of a graph that shows the different amounts of authority and responsibility given to the principal and to the staff. Styles to the left in Figure 3 give more power to the principal, while those to the right give more to staff. It should be emphasized that none of these styles is always any better or worse than others; all are productive and satisfying styles for both principal and staff in appropriate situations.[2] Principals in the cases used the full variety of styles, sometimes effectively and sometimes not.

CASE 1: AN ADMINISTRATIVE ENTREPRENEUR

Joe Lyons was described as having concern for children and ideas to help them, as an advisor and helper, as stressing mutual expectations and group agreements in participatory decision-making, and as sounding out ideas with his staff.

Style: initially *testing* or *consulting* and then *delegating* and *joining*.

CASE 2: MOVING BACKSTAGE

Paul Harrison was described as putting students' interests first, as strong in focusing on goals, purposeful, methodical, sometimes autocratic and perhaps unyielding and tactless, but also as responsive, supportive, and democratic.

Style: a variety of styles that fit the occasion, ranging from *telling* to *delegating*.

CASE 3: INSIGHT AND SKILLS

Staff members described Martin Lawrence's style with terms such as: high-energy, acquisitive in seeking resources, supporting the project verbally and modelling good participant behaviors, having high status with the central office,

---

[2]Asking the question, "What is the best leadership style?" is like asking "What are the best clothes?" The answer, of course, is that it depends on what you're doing—playing tennis, painting the house, or attending a formal dinner. No one set of clothes is always "best," only appropriate or inappropriate for the occasion.

FIGURE 3

Authority and Responsibility Relative to Leadership Styles

Adapted from Robert Tannenbaum and Warren H. Schmidt, "How to Choose a Leadership Pattern," *Harvard Business Review*, *51*(3), May-June 1973, p. 164.

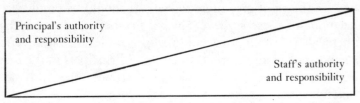

Principal's authority and responsibility

Staff's authority and responsibility

Telling Selling Testing Consulting Delegating Joining

- *Telling:* The principal identifies a problem, considers alternative solutions, chooses one, and tells the staff what they are to do. They may be considered but do not participate directly in decisions.
- *Selling:* The principal makes the decision but tries to persuade the staff to accept it, for instance by pointing out how organizational goals have been considered and how they will benefit from carrying out the decision.
- *Testing:* The principal identifies the problem and proposes a tentative solution, asking for reactions of staff who will implement it. The principal considers those reactions and then makes the decision.
- *Consulting:* Staff have a chance to influence the decision from the beginning. The principal presents the problem and information about it. Staff are then invited to offer solutions and the principal then selects the one he or she considers most promising.
- *Delegating:* The principal assigns decision-making responsibility and authority to the staff, perhaps reserving a power of veto or modification. Usually the principal gives a charge that describes specifically the limits of authority, solution requirements, and the range of acceptable solutions.
- *Joining:* The manager participates equally with other staff members in decisions and actions, wielding no more or less power than other members of the group.

---

having good contacts, and active in negotiating with environmental pressures and resources.

Style: again, a variety of styles ranging from *testing* to *joining*.

CASE 4: SUCCESS IN A VERY SMALL SCHOOL

Head teacher Pamela Bishop was described in many complimentary ways. People used words like positive attitude, clarity of goals, honesty, directness, willing to try new ideas, concern for teachers' feelings, solving problems, respecting confidences, and the like.

Style: following *testing* and *consulting* at the beginning of the project, she relied heavily on *delegating* and *joining* because the staff took considerable responsibility.

CASE 5: WATERTOWN

Descriptions of Bill Foster's style were varied and seemingly contradictory. Faculty saw him as oriented to curriculum and academic standards, as "autocratic" (but usually only in comparison with the previous principal and only when the situation merited forcefulness), concerned with relationships and personal interaction, building trust, a "we" man rather than an "I" man, recognizing teachers' contributions, laissez faire, charismatic, low key but dynamic.

Style: Foster obviously used the full range of styles, but he was not perceived as inconsistent. Instead, he seemed to know how to match style to expectation and situation; perhaps the key to understanding his style is appreciating his comment that "the project molds the principal."

CASE 6: A COMMUNITY PROJECT

There is little information about George Hanna's style. While staff said they trusted him and his decisions, they also felt a lack of leadership and direction.

Style: Hanna's main style, *delegation*, did not seem well matched to the faculty's expectations.

CASE 7: HARVESTING A VOLUNTEER CROP

Warren Redford was generally described as a facilitator although strong in advocating the program and shaping the participation of community volunteers to meet the school's needs.

Style: In contrast to Hanna, Redford's *delegating* style seemed to be in accord with the staff and the situation.

CASE 8: A MIXED BAG

Recall the many discrepancies in this case. While the project director cited instances of effective leadership and thoughtfulness, others used words such as: withdrawal, no data base for

121

decisions, unilateral decision-making, a shrinking circle of advisors, no consultation, "I'm not sure what he does," insensitive, naive about involving people, not good interpersonal skills, and values that seem to conflict with the heart of the project. The researcher described his style as that of a college professor giving a lecture illustrated with a wall chart.

Style: It was apparently a *telling* style (mandating the project in the face of faculty resistance) that brought the project to the school, but Flood seemed to give mixed signals of both continued *telling* (in various room changes) and a *delegation* that appeared to the staff as abdication of interest and leadership.

CASE 9: STRESS

Although Jeremy Watson was well liked and teachers thought he ran a good school, project staff felt he lacked skills and organization to manage the project effectively, and that he was too tied up in administrivia to exert educational leadership. He saw himself as a facilitator, but they wanted a director.

Style: After the *consulting* or *testing* style used at first (when he suggested the reading program as a way to cope with overcrowding), Watson's *delegating* style let the staff enjoy the latitude they had to operate the program but it also prompted them to wish that he had given them more guidance.

CASE 10: TWILIGHT OF A PROJECT

Principal Eric Horton was described as variable, informal, not authoritative (does that mean not authoritarian?), not direct, laissez faire, apathetic, relaxed, and humanistic. He saw himself as a facilitator rather than a director.

Style: Horton's style seemed to be on the right-hand side of the continuum, toward *consulting, delegating,* or *joining* styles which were less forceful than the staff wanted.

CASE 11: I NEVER DID SEE THE PRINCIPAL

Since it is unclear how the decision to adopt the project was made, we cannot assign a style to principal Tom Palmer's actions in that instance. Both the principal and vice-principal seemed to share a laissez-faire, live-and-let-live leadership style. Teachers regarded the administrators as perhaps willing to help but as not having the content or process skills to do so, and as not having a real interest in curriculum in any event.

Style: It is the absence of both leadership and style that marks this project: perhaps the best characterization of the style is "abdication."

At the risk of repetition, a variety of styles led to success and the key was how well the principal's style matched staff expectations and task demands. Generally, "middle-range" styles (testing, consulting, delegating) worked better than the extremes of telling or joining (or abdicating). Other themes emerge from the descriptions:

- In successful projects, the principal was seen as having a strong focus on curriculum, academic standards, and students; in less successful projects, the staff felt that attention to administrivia got in the way of educational leadership.
- Principals in successful projects usually worked to keep a focus on clear and shared goals and clear expectations about roles.
- Attention to teachers' feelings, individual needs, and giving strokes and reinforcement was often mentioned in successful projects.
- Nearly all principals—especially the successful ones— did a variety of supporting tasks such as acquiring resources, negotiating with the central office, and even preparing materials. (Sometimes the principal is the coach, and sometimes the waterboy.)
- The head teacher's directness and honesty were as appreciated as Flood's mixed messages were distrusted.
- Teachers appreciated instances of the principal's initiative, whether they took the form of getting the project going or stopping by occasionally to ask how things were going.

123

Our findings verify what others have found. Jennings (in Hersey and Blanchard, 1977: 89), for instance, concludes, "Fifty years of study have failed to produce one personality trait or set of qualities that can be used to discriminate leaders and non-leaders." Nor is it likely that the "ideal leadership style" *will* be discovered: "While one can never say that something is impossible, and while someone may well discover the all-purpose leadership style or behavior at some future time, our own data and those which have come out of sound research by other investigators do not promise such miraculous curves" (Fiedler, in Hersey and Blanchard, 1977: 130). In fact, the best current research supports our earlier statements that the "best" leadership style depends on being adaptable: "The more managers adapt their style of leader behavior to meet the particular situation and the needs of their followers, the more effective they will tend to be in reaching personal and organizational goals" (Hersey, in Hersey and Blanchard, 1977: 101).

Some faculties appreciated what appears to be some "authoritarian" (telling) behaviors by the principal, while in other schools the same kind of behavior was resented. Some staffs felt very comfortable with the principal's delegation, while to other faculties that action signalled a lack of interest. We will discuss ways of matching leadership style to expectations and the situation in Chapter 4.

Life Cycles of Funded Projects and the Principal's Role

We did not set out to look at the life cycles of projects and what principals did, but when we visited the schools we heard people say, "in the beginning, the principal . . ." or "when we were developing materials, the principal . . . " and "when the project was over, she . . . ." It became clear that effective principals did different things at different times and that the match between the stage of the project and the principal's behavior was important.

We found that projects had common life cycles that could be more or less defined. That should not be surprising, since in most cases the projects were funded by federal agencies which usually specify expectations for various stages of work. We were able to fit the life cycles into four stages: planning and initiation, building a temporary system, development and implementation, and ending and institutionalization.[3] We next describe each of the four stages and principals' behaviors in each.

PLANNING AND INITIATION

All projects except one required a formal proposal to a funding agency. Some required only brief statements for planners at local districts, while others specified lengthy documents with detailed scopes of work and management plans. Funders generally wanted statements of the need addressed by the project, of goals and objectives, and of how the goals would be achieved by a sequence of activities.

Principals varied greatly in their involvement during this stage. Some were the prime movers: they identified the need, convinced others of its importance, and wrote the proposal single-handedly. At the opposite extreme, one principal learned about the project only when he showed up for his first day at work!

The most successful projects had principals who were intensely involved during the initial stage. Take the example of Joe Lyons in Case 1, who concluded from student test scores that some students from low-income families were losing as much as a year in reading skills during the summer. He contacted an acquaintance in an oil company and negotiated a small sum for a special program. Once the money was acquired, he gained support from staff and others by discussing the program at faculty meetings and social gatherings. Before

---

[3]Of course, developing descriptive schemes to describe stages of change is a favorite pastime of researchers, so a vast array of categories, stages, and descriptive schemes exists. Examples are Havelock (1973), Lewin (in Franch and Bell, 1978), among others, and Runkel, Schmuck, Arends, and Francisco (1979). The reader is undoubtedly familiar with others. This one worked for us.

long he had persuaded others of the need for the program and had faculty actively involved in planning the program.[4]

Every successful project did not command this much investment by the principal in planning and initiation, especially those in which others had considerable energy to give to it. But it was more usual than not that successful projects had principals who were involved in the beginning. It appeared critical that the principal agreed with the project's concept, provided some input into the proposal, and began communicating his or her support and enthusiasm.

In another case, the principal acted mainly to involve others and to link them with resources from the district and funding agency. Teachers in Case 3 believed their project got off to a good start because of the many, many meetings that Lawrence had had with parents and teachers before the proposal was submitted. As the Rand studies found (Greenwood, Mann, and McLaughlin, 1975) project success was more likely when participants formed a large enough "critical mass" to provide mutual support and share ideas.

Among the kinds of helpful behaviors reported to us were: the principal held faculty meetings to interpret and clarify project goals; he wrote the proposal because he was dissatisfied with the existing program; the principal used data from test scores to identify the problem; the principal supervised proposal preparation and negotiated budget with the funding agency. Less successful projects were those in which the principal unilaterally decided to bring it to the school or in which the principal had no hand in the planning and initiation stage.

Generally, the successful cases illustrate the Rand finding (Berman and McLaughlin, 1975) that success is due in part to a receptive institutional setting characterized by a problem-solving attitude rather than opportunism for available funds. In many cases the principal created that receptiveness by leading discussions that generated a shared awareness of the problem.

[4]Lyons is a good illustration of what House (1974) calls the "entrepreneur," an advocate who works within the system to bring about change.

Successful cases also illustrate the Fullan and Pomfret (1975) finding that successful principals provided ways for teachers to define their own needs and find their own solutions.

In short, active initiation on the part of the principal was generally required, but it had been the kind of leadership that brought others into the process of defining the problem and creating the solution.

BUILDING A TEMPORARY SYSTEM

Implementing the projects' proposals required that people be brought together in a "temporary system" to plan and carry out project activities. The term "temporary system" comes from Miles (1964: Chapter 19), who points out that they have special characteristics, strengths, and problems that distinguish them from permanent systems in the school such as departments, management teams, and the like. Among the more important characteristics, they are *temporary*—there are definite time limits on the life of the group. They are formed to deal with specific, limited goals. They are "adjuncts" to the normal school structure, so they must work out problems of interacting with permanent people and structures in the school. Since they usually have some sort of psychological or physical isolation, they are protected somewhat from the routine pressures of the system but also may have difficulty in making links with the permanent structure. The new roles and tasks of the temporary group are not those of the permanent system, so they must be created by the group's members. New groups do not have clear "rules of the game," channels of communication among members and between the group and the permanent system, and established ways of working together, so they also must be created. Finally, temporary systems typically encounter frustration arising from overly ambitious plans, unrealistic goals, and the lack of both task and relationship skills needed for productive and satisfying work.

The eleven projects had a variety of temporary systems. Six added new staff especially for the project, in three cases the

127

role of the staff or an individual was redefined (as when a teacher was appointed project director), while two used existing staff in new ways, in effect creating a temporary system by creating new roles, relationships, goals, and ways of working together.

Principals varied greatly in their abilities and willingness to perform the tasks needed to build this temporary system. Some, such as Martin Lawrence in Case 3, excelled at this task. He knew the importance of finding good staff, and fought with central office superiors to conduct a national search for one staff member. He was skilled in bringing parents and teachers together to generate the common vision and commitment the project needed. And he was forceful with the funders in negotiating the autononomy and resources they needed. Others lacked the skills or did not take time to insure that the temporary system was established. Some were naive about the symbolic value of space and the effect of new resources and people in the school. Still others did not select project participants carefully and thus missed those who might have had the energy and commitment needed for the project.

Principals took a variety of roles in relation to building the temporary system. Some were intensely involved, while others delegated the crucial tasks, permitting staff to carry out start-up activities. Yet others virtually ignored the projects. The most successful projects seemed to be those in which the principal took an active role, both in dealing with the tasks of the project and establishing the temporary system and its relationships.

Behaviors that seemed to be crucial to a project's success included moving quickly and surely to hire, assign, or recruit project staff; securing space that was central within the school; negotiating with the funding agency about budget and expectations; making financial arrangements with the central office; selling the idea to the superintendent; convincing colleagues in other schools that the project deserved their support; and helping to create the temporary systems.

Principals supported the temporary systems in a vareity of ways, from preparing materials they would need to providing (or arranging for) training, securing resources—such as funds for a summer proposal-writing team—and keeping a strong focus on the goals and tasks they were to accomplish.

In two cases which were unsuccessful, necessary tasks were not done. The principal in Case 11 apparently never established a committed and competent temporary system, while Jim Flood in Case 8 created antagonisms between the project and the teaching staff at the outset by his arbitrary assignment of the project's space.

The key leadership style at this stage is *delegation*, a turning over of authority and responsibility to the persons who will carry out the project's core tasks, but the delegation must be accompanied by a clear mandate and continued support, helpfulness, and interest.

DEVELOPMENT AND IMPLEMENTATION

In this third stage of projects, the tasks were the creation of materials, testing new teaching practices in classrooms, and some type of inservice training for teachers and others expected to behave in new ways. While in the first two stages the main tasks were those of "getting ready" to do it, this is the "doing it" stage, and the principal's role changes accordingly. Principals in this stage generally stepped back from leadership roles in which they exercised considerable initiative to managerial roles in which they supported and helped those who were working on the project's central tasks. As we shall discuss at greater length in Chapter 4, the principal's concern at this stage was less with "task" issues and more with "relationship" issues.

Again, principals varied greatly in their involvement during this stage. Their involvement was influenced in part by the size or complexity of the project and the school. In very small schools and in projects that had no extra monies for staff, principals remained very much involved. Tasks they performed ranged from ordering or developing materials to conducting inservice training. In larger schools and in projects in which project staff were hired, principals normally pulled away from day-to-day involvement with few negative consequences.

A pattern in successful projects was for principals to remain interested, taking the initiative to keep informed about the project and ready to provide problem-solving around obstacles that arose, but to turn over the project to others. We have called this "moving backstage." Successful principals seemed to know that at some point it was time to turn "their baby" over to others. The key thing was to know when staff were ready—with both the commitment and the ability—to take on those tasks.

Even while turning over the project to others, successful principals remained involved in supporting roles. People told us of principals' activities: He attended many project events, such as potlucks and movies, at the school. He guided inservice efforts on supervision techniques for unit leaders. The principal attended inservice training as a participant. She did the administrative work to insure that supplies were there when we needed them, she always knew how the program was functioning in classrooms, and she took pains to tell her teachers how she felt about what they were doing. Foster gave recognition to both project teachers and the good, hard-working teacher who isn't involved that much.

Less successful projects were those in which the principal's delegation of project tasks was seen as a withdrawal of interest and support, or as letting routines and administrivia divert attention from the project.

The development and implementation stage can be frustrating for principals, since it is the stage in which the necessity of accomplishing goals by working *through* others is most apparent. The rewards are less directly those of seeing tasks accomplished by one's own efforts, and more those of seeing others accomplish tasks with one's support. At the same time, many demands compete for the principal's time and attention. It was in this stage that project staff most frequently raised

130

complaints that the principal seemed less accessible or interested in the project.

ENDING AND INSTITUTIONALIZATION

Most agencies that funded projects we studied were interested in making permanent changes in schools; they intended that new practices introduced by the project would remain in operation after outside funding was withdrawn. Most called this institutionalization—making permanent something that is new. As in other stages, the principal's behavior was critical here. In almost every instance in which we studied a project near the end of its life, the principal had decided what was to remain.[5]

The most important behavior seemed to be the principal's commitment to continuing some project activities and the ability to find resources to continue them. For instance, in one project (not one we described in Chapter 2) all agreed that it was touch and go for some time whether the new curriculum would remain in the school after the project ended. The chief action was the principal's decision to keep it and her ability to persuade department chairpersons to assign regular staff to the new curriculum. In that same project, the principal's leadership in writing a proposal to a new funding agency was critical in continuing a community education program. A similar example can be found in the instance of Joe Lyons (Case 1), who convinced parents to support the summer reading program with money from bake sales for the year after we studied the project.

One case that bears special mention is Case 10, in which it was questionable whether the project should have been attempted at all. The question of whether to continue the moribund project was not faced until the second year, when the principal approached the project director with his concerns and perceptions. The issue raised here is that sometimes a wise decision to abandon a project may be as helpful to a

---

[5]We lack information about ending and institutionalization for several projects, since we studied them before they ended.

school as any other action the principal may take. Sarason (1971: 217–18) comments:

> in different settings one may very well answer the questions of where to start rather differently, a consequence those who need to follow a recipe will find unsatisfactory because there is no one place to start. Still another consequence is that one may decide indeed that there are times when one should decide *to start nowhere.* That is, the minimal conditions required for that change to take hold, regardless of where one starts, are not present . . . the decision not to proceed with a particular change, far from being an evasion, forces one to consider *what other kinds of changes have to take place before the minimal conditions can be said to exist.*

That observation also obviously applies to Case 11, in which no one (except perhaps the district specialist) really wanted the project. We shall have more to say about recognizing conditions for readiness in Chapter 4.

On the one hand, as project activities become incorporated into the normal routine of the school, the principal's activity presumably decreases. On the other hand, "institutionalization" also represents a new stage in which many of the issues of what is to be done, who will do it, what resources are needed, and other issues from earlier stages are played through again.

Principals' Behaviors That Facilitated or Restrained Project Accomplishments

We found that project staff, teachers, and principals we interviewed consistently noted several behaviors that helped the projects. When principals took those actions, the projects were generally successful. When principals did not take those actions, or when the principal's behavior was unhelpful or restraining, the project was less likely to be successful.

Some of those behaviors were directed toward accomplishing project tasks, while others were directed toward building staff relationships or support for the project. This distinction has many names, such as "task vs. maintenance," "content vs. process," and so on. N. R. F. Maier (1970) calls attention to the dual needs of "quality" (of the solution) and "acceptance"

132

(by group members) if solutions are to be implemented. We have termed those two sets of behaviors "task" and "relationship," since those labels are used by Hersey and Blanchard (1977), whose work we will rely on in Chapter 4. The eight behaviors fall equally into the two categories, as illustrated in Figure 4. Those behaviors seemed to cut across project stages. While some behaviors are more closely related to some stages than to others, it was generally true that all the behaviors found some place in nearly every stage of the project.

FIGURE 4
Categories of Behaviors

Task	Relationship
1 Understanding the central concept of the project	5 Achieving role clarity
2 Commitment to the concept and vision of the project	6 Encouraging involvement and participation
3 Negotiating with competing environmental pressures	7 Providing social support and active participation
4 Using and allocating resources	8 Providing feedback and evaluation

This is an appropriate time for a reminder that it is simplistic to view the principal as the all-powerful sole determiner of the project's fate. Many other actors and agencies influence that outcome. But their actions seem in many ways to hinge on the principal, who is at the focal point (or firing line!) of the project. The principal orchestrates much of the work of others.

UNDERSTANDING THE CENTRAL CONCEPT
OF THE PROJECT

Although not in every instance, in several cases we saw that staff had expectations that the principal be knowledgeable about the concept of the project. When he or she wasn't, we heard comments such as: the principal lacked knowledge of the project's content and procedures; the principal lacked understanding of the project; the principal didn't know enough about it to explain it to the funding agency. In more successful

133

projects we heard: the principal is extremely knowledgeable about community resource use and can train others; the principal taught supervision techniques to unit leaders; he has the respect of teachers because he understands the project; the principal knows how to operate federal projects; the principal edited the final product.

Normally the expectation was not that the principal be the expert; expertise generally rested with the project staff. However, staff wanted the principal to understand the project in enough detail to communicate their efforts to others.

Sarason (1971: 129ff) points out the dilemma of the principal who has aspirations of educational leadership but must work with project staff who may have greater expertise than he or she: "The consequence of this interaction is that the principal is constantly wrestling with the problem of leadership with the feeling . . . that he is losing the battle, that he is not the leader he expected to be, or would like to be, or that others expect him to be." Our findings suggest that principals need *not* have this worry, that teachers will *not* think less of them if their expertise is less than the project staff's. What is needed (and expected) is that the principal have enough of a "speaking acquaintance" with what the project is all about to perform various supporting tasks.

Principals were called on to act as advocates for the project to various audiences (and to defend it from critics), to anticipate needs for materials, and to keep the staff focused on goals. These and similar tasks required that principals have a basic understanding of the project and how it worked.

COMMITMENT TO THE CONCEPT AND VISION OF THE PROJECT

In some cases, it was the principal's vision of what the school needed that went into the proposal and he or she was the prime mover in getting the project started. In other instances the principal inherited the project from others or was called on to support the energy and vision of others. While it was not always essential that the principal initiate the vision, it

134

was critical that the principal feel a genuine commitment to the project and that his or her enthusiasm be demonstrated and communicated to others.

Sarason (1971: 130), as usual, pinpoints the dilemma:

> . . . regardless of whether or not the principal likes the proposed changes he is in large part responsible for implementing these changes *in fact and in spirit* . . . When he is not in favor of the proposed change, his dilemma may be simultaneously increased and decreased: increased because he must do something he does not favor, and decreased because he does not feel personally responsible for the change and can so represent himself to others . . .

Our advice—to which we will return often—is that principals avoid that dilemma wherever possible.[6] Because teachers depend on the principal for cues about what is important and what kinds of effort will be rewarded and approved, they will quickly recognize a lack of commitment and will act accordingly.

In projects that were going smoothly, we heard from project staff and teachers statements such as: the principal is a strong advocate of project goals; the principal is positive about the program; he presented a positive image to the staff on project objectives; she is enthusiastic about the concept of the project; and the principal promoted the value of the project.

In other projects people told us: the principal did not write the proposal and never really agreed with the idea; the principal was hired after the proposal was written and didn't like the project's goals; when the project is discussed, the principal acts bored.

It is clear that when the chief administrator of the school does not believe in the project, teachers and others have an uphill struggle against strong odds to make it succeed. Verbal support and expressions of commitment are needed but are not by themselves enough. Staff need to see the principal

---

[6]Of course, avoiding the dilemma is *not* always possible; there are numerous instances in which the principal must enforce mandates and decisions from the district, state, or federal agencies. But when participation in an externally funded project is voluntary, the dilemma should be avoidable.

making an active effort to accomodate and support the change. Recall the finding by the SOC researchers (Runkel, Schmuck, Arends, and Francisco, 1979: 108) that it was important for the principal to "support changes in the roles of others by making reciprocal changes in his or her own role. (Change is much more difficult when the administrator says, 'You go ahead and change, but don't expect me to do so.')." Case 8 is perhaps our best illustration of what happens when the principal gives out confusing signals and when statements of support are contradicted by actions that seem to signal withdrawal of interest and support.

A distinction that is useful is what Argyris and Schon (1974) call the difference between "espoused theory" and "theory-in-action." Espoused theory is what the person says she or he believes—the kind of answer one would get on a questionnaire about values. Theory-in-action is the set of beliefs that an observer would attribute to the person by watching what he or she actually does. Teachers watch principals closely and are quick to respond to discrepancies between espoused theory and theory-in-action. Whether their interpretation is correct or not is not the point; the point is that people act on *their interpretations* of the principal's behavior, which may not be what the principal intended. We have several cases in which the principal saw himself as delegating responsibility to the staff and allowing them to take ownership in the project, but teachers perceived those actions as signals of a lack of interest and support, a withdrawal from the project. The same actions can give rise to different interpretations, depending on who does the interpreting.

In a sense, verbal statements are promises, but action is what delivers on the promise. Statements of support mean little if the staff does not see the principal taking pains to arrange his or her schedule to make time for the project, fighting with the central office to expedite delivery of supplies when they are needed, and so on. Swaab (1972: 57) concludes: "What this says to me is that the principal needs to set the norm-changing model for the school. It does no good for him to encourage teachers to take risks when he takes none. Nor is it productive to exhort teachers to trust each other when he is distrustful . . . ."

The message, we think, is clear and blunt: teachers will quickly see through a pretense of support, so "practice what you preach."

NEGOTIATING WITH COMPETING ENVIRONMENTAL PRESSURES

Schools exist in a highly political and sometimes capricious environment. Many groups—educators, parents, students, and special interest coalitions—vie for a say about the purposes and processes of schools. Most innovative efforts upset the fragile stability of the school and its environment: "the introduction of an important change does not and cannot have the same significance for the different groupings comprising the setting . . . one consequence is that there will be groups that will feel obligated to obstruct, divert, or defeat the proposed change" (Sarason, 1971: 59). Dealing with the many groups and their preferences or demands is one of the most difficult tasks in a project, and it is one that inevitably falls to the principal.

In successful projects, we heard comments such as: The principal provided training and orientation to community volunteers. He held meetings with parents to alert them to the problem. The principal formed a group of interested teachers prior to funding. He went to bat for the project with the school board. He tried to get political support from other principals for the curriculum reform. The principal spent 80 to 90 percent of his time the first year doing public relations for the project.

For instance, project staff in Case 3 consistently mentioned Lawrence's willingness to run interference for them at the central office and to acquire resources from the district. They saw him as a person who knew his way around the district, who could "get on the phone and speak to the right people"

137

without being shuffled around from office to office as often happened to them.

The head teacher's role in Case 4 as a mediator and conciliator was often mentioned. The project generated some resistance from parents and that opposition was supported by some members of the school board. She was credited with handling most of the criticism and interpreting the program to its critics.

Though we found no project that was scuttled by environmental pressures (a possible exception is Case 10, which had a community in decline and turmoil and a superintendent who was viewed as varying between "non-supportive and negative"). We found cases in which the project was helped by a critical intervention with some disgruntled faction.

There were several ways in which the principal helped the project by dealing with environmental pressures. One was by serving as a liaison or linker between the project and the outside world. For instance, some principals negotiated expectations with the funding agency. Another was by serving as an advocate or spokesperson, advocating the project before a variety of audiences. Another was by being a "buffer" to protect the project from criticism and giving the staff room to operate. Another was by acquiring the resources and support from the district needed to support the project.

USING AND ALLOCATING RESOURCES

Externally funded projects require a variety of tangible and intangible resources to make them operate; some are provided by funds from the granting agencies, while others must be gotten from local sources. Runkel, Schmuck, Arends, and Francisco (1979: 125) list tangible resources such as services, goods, and money, and intangible resources such as information, status, and affection. How principals acquired, used, and allocated resources was consistently reported to us as critical to the success of a project.

On the facilitating side we heard: The principal obtained money from the district to hire a team of teachers to write the

138

proposal. He persuaded the publisher to conduct a free inservice for teachers. The principal opened up the building to the community. She used resources from the project to achieve the multicultural objectives of the school. He convinced the business office to simplify paperwork to facilitate hiring. The principal assigned the project to a room that was conveniently located. The principal shortened the school day twice a month and used the time for planning. The principal found non-project funds for teachers to visit other schools.

Some principals had excellent skills in acquiring and allocating resources. They seemed to understand, too, the sensitivities associated with integrating people, space, and things into the on-going school routine. Martin Lawrence in Case 3 was seen as one who was always reaching out to get resources for the school: "Whereas some administrators are afraid to have outside people in the building, Lawrence grabs anyone he sees if he thinks it will add to the school's instructional program."

But we also heard, in schools where things were not going well: The principal did not seek the district resources needed to support the project. He assigned the project to a room in a wing of the building that was not accessible. He did not give special administrative favors to help the project. The principal assigned an inexperienced teacher to the project. He hired a non-teacher to be the project director.

Some intangible resources the principal can acquire from outside the project are the approval of the school board and community, clear expectations from the funders to give project staff a clear direction, and support from colleagues in other buildings. Other intangible resources can be provided only by the principal. That is especially true of the principal's own time, attention, support, and hugs or encouraging words.

The job of allocating and acquiring resources is unique to the principal. Teachers and project staff rarely have the position, mobility, time, authority to make decisions, or knowledge of the system's procedures to get resources into the building and then distribute them where they are needed.

In several cases it was clear that the goods or services provided by the principal were more important for their symbolic value than for their actual use. That is most clearly illustrated in Case 8, in which the principal first took a room away from a popular teacher and gave it to the project, but then later moved the project to a "closet" on the third floor. While the room assignments were of course themselves important, the ways they were handled seemed to become rallying points and battlegrounds, symbolic fields on which tensions between principal and staff were played out.

ACHIEVING ROLE CLARITY

We were struck by the fact that in successful cases both the principal and others described his or her actions in very similar terms and they agreed on what behaviors were helpful and unhelpful. In less successful cases, we found a lack of that agreement and a significant lack of clarity about what the principal did or was supposed to do. Those observations alerted us to the importance of achieving clear roles for the principal and gaining acceptance for performing those roles.

"Role" is usually defined as a set of expectations about how an individual in a position is supposed to behave. It is not surprising that there was a good deal of confusion and conflict about what principals in these projects were supposed to do. For one thing, job descriptions do not adequately describe the demands of the job:

> The role of the principal cannot be understood by a listing or description of what he can or cannot do, if for no other reason than conditions change and new problems arise. Any job description of a principal consists essentially of a set of generalizations which, if anything, states or implies the *minimum* limits or scope of the position. It does not describe the maximum limits or scope of the position. For example, the job description may state that the principal is responsible for the quality of instruction in the school; it will not state the myriad of ways by which the principal could or should discharge this responsibility. (Sarason, 1971: 141)

Second, externally funded projects are relatively new in

schools, and many of the actions needed to carry them out are not the sort called for in routine operations of the school. Generally, problems about the role of the principal in these cases fell into two categories.

Role Confusion.—In some projects, principals reported feeling confused and uncomfortable about their role in relation to the project. One principal wanted to be involved and helpful but was fearful that taking too active a part would undermine the project director. Another principal reported that she was never sure how she was supposed to behave and felt unsure of herself during visits from the project's federal monitor.

In contrast, several principals were "old hands" at externally funded projects, were clear about what needed to be done, and felt confident in their ability to do it.

Perhaps the extreme case of role confusion in project leadership was Case 11, in which no one was clear as to who was running the show. In contrast, Joe Lyons in Case 1 performed a wide variety of tasks, but both he and project staff described his roles in very similar terms.

Role Conflict.—In several projects we heard complaints that the principal was playing his role poorly. Teachers in these projects said: The principal allows administrative duties to compete with project needs. The principal never comes to our project meetings. The principal gave all the responsibility to the project director and doesn't care anymore. He is too far removed from the project and is not accessible to the staff.

In those same projects, we heard principals say, "The project runs well without me, because teachers have a lot of ownership in it. Besides, I have a hundred things going on in this building and I can't do everything myself."

Those comments clearly signal incompatible and conflicting expectations about what principals should do. Teachers and project staff made demands for more of the principal's attention while he or she was saying, "My job is like that of an air traffic controller—there is more to do than I can possibly attend to." Things went better in projects in which these conflicts were resolved and in which staff and principal had com-

141

mon expectations about the appropriate behavior and involvement of the principal.

The most pervasive and stressful conflicts had to do with how much direct involvement the principal should have with the project and with whether the principal should be directing and initiating or should be a facilitator and helper. One project director felt that the principal spent too much time "putting out fires" and not enough time on the project. Another saw the school's administrators as too harassed by other duties to attend to the project. Many persons thought their principals let administrivia take too much time from educational and project leadership.

Principals also felt role conflicts. One noted the dilemma of the need "for principals to confront teachers and provide leadership toward achievement of goals, but also have faculty participation in the direction and way to proceed." He also felt the conflict between his role as a planner and his role in day-to-day operations. Even in Case 8, in which so many of the principal's actions seemed detrimental to the project, the question is open. As the field researcher queried:

> It is interesting to wonder whether Flood, with his experience and his pride in teaching administrative theory at the college level, was truly unaware of the value systems operating in his school. Was it a case of administrative overload? Was he, as the staff believed, uninvolved and uncommitted to the project's goals and activities? Or were they simply too dependent on the power of the principal to take the initiative to carry the effort themselves?

In many ways, role conflict is the hallmark of the modern principalship. There are more demands on the principal's time than can be met by one person. Students, faculty, parents, the district, the federal government, and a host of other actors press their claims—often forcibly—upon the principal's attention. The externally funded project can easily become simply another one of these demands.

Principals who want to be educational leaders can be in a difficult position when their aspirations are not supported by superiors or subordinates. In most school bureaucracies it is paperwork and not peoplework that is rewarded. But principals will always have more demands on their time than they can satisfy, and their task (admittedly a difficult one) is to decide which of those demands are important to meet.

There are no easy answers. The key lies in the principal's ability to manage time, energy, and attention according to priorities about what is important.

There is also no one right answer as to what role the principal should play in the project. As a teacher in Case 5 observed: "But what a good principal is really depends on the location. The community requires certain things of a principal and sometimes a principal may have those characteristics and sometimes not. Most faculty welcome good strong leadership but also want to be involved in the decision-making structure, particularly when the decision is about curriculum."

ENCOURAGING INVOLVEMENT AND PARTICIPATION

Most projects were not written by teachers, but in every instance teachers' involvement was needed in carrying out project activities. Sometimes only a few teachers participated, while in other schools the entire faculty took part. In some projects involvement was voluntary, while in others all teachers were required to act in new ways. Bringing teachers on board after the project was launched and gaining their commitment to it taxed the abilities of most principals.

Teachers reported many helpful things that principals did: The principal encouraged faculty participation in providing direction for the project. He explained to the regular faculty how the project would benefit them. Foster got the teachers to look at their own teaching behavior. He encouraged participation in inservice events. The principal arranged staff visits to other schools. He selected unit leaders and helped them develop and operate as a team. She allowed the staff to own problems with the program. The principal involved the staff in joint decisions to bring the project into the school.

At other times we heard of less helpful actions: The principal did not encourage (or require) teacher participation. He

143

accepted teacher resistance and even encouraged it. The principal did not seek teacher involvement until after the project was well under way.

Success, we should note, did *not* depend on whether participation was optional or mandatory. Two projects that allowed optional participation were successful, while one was not. Several which required total staff involvement were successful, while others were not. Apparently, *how* teachers were involved had a greater impact than whether their participation was required or voluntary.

In most successful cases, principals involved teachers very early in the planning, often before a proposal was submitted. Joe Lyons in Case 1, for instance, spent time "planting seeds" at faculty meetings and social gatherings, asking people, "What do you think of this idea?" Martin Lawrence in Case 3 held meetings of parents and teachers to create awareness of the problem and to initiate a search for solutions. Paul Harrison in Case 2 persevered through two unsuccessful attempts to gain the staff's commitment, finally succeeding with a strategy that recognized teachers' experience and their loyalty to their departments.

We think that early involvement is important for this reason. Externally funded projects are solutions to problems. (Recall the Rand finding that more successful projects were those that addressed widely felt problems rather than ones that opportunistically sought additional funds.) If teachers do not share an awareness of the problem and desire to do something about it, they are unlikely to commit themselves to the project. Some unsuccessful projects seemed to be solutions for which there was no problem; Case 11 is perhaps the clearest example of that. Acceptance of the problem is one of the crucial conditions of readiness we shall stress in Chapter 4.

Successful principals found a variety of ways to encourage faculty participation. Some arranged schedules to make participation in inservice convenient for the staff. Others participated in the inservice themselves and modeled good participant behaviors. Still others provided incentives and rewards.

144

Bill Foster in Case 5 worked hard to create a decision-making structure that involved his faculty. Others performed supporting tasks that freed teachers to concentrate on the project; Joe Lyons in Case 1 was described as "bus driver, downtown tour guide, tent-pole setter and camp cook." Finally, many principals exerted special efforts to build good working relationships with teachers. That action was one key to the success of Pamela Bishop in Case 4. The field researcher described the efforts of Bill Foster in Case 5:

> Negative teachers who thought allocation of resources for the magnet program were disproportionate (magnet got more money for fewer students than did other academic programs) were part of his early problem. Initially, he had a fair amount of intolerance toward faculty members, and rather than taking the time to find out why they were not cooperating, he shied away from dealing with a close relationship that the job required. He was quick to say that he thought one of the things he learned from the project was the need to develop these complicated relationships.

Less successful principals did not seem to put out this kind of effort. We visited many projects in which the principal's delegation of work to the staff was seen as a withdrawal of support and interest. Some teachers told us, "The principal never asked teachers what they were doing." Other principals apparently did not know how to involve faculty, as in the school in which we heard, "The principal attempted to win support by offering inservice activities viewed by teachers as inappropriate and poorly timed."

Our findings about teacher involvement support many of the conclusions of the Rand study. Greenwood, Mann, and McLaughlin (1975) reported that successful projects had continuous planning and frequent reassessment of methods and goals. It was found that intangible psychological incentives were more effective in eliciting teachers' involvement than were tangible incentives such as extra pay or credit on the district's pay scale. Leaders of successful projects relied on a flexible administrative approach and kept communication channels open so that project participants could deal with unanticipated problems as they arose.

145

The critical issues seemed to be the extent to which teachers were involved in defining the problem addressed by the project, whether principals found ways to encourage participation through various incentives, and principals' continuing demonstrations of interest and support.

PROVIDING SOCIAL SUPPORT AND ACTIVE PARTICIPATIONS

The behaviors most often mentioned as contributing to the fate of a project were what we have termed "providing social support and active participation." These behaviors ranged all the way from supplying resources at critical times to a warm hug at a difficult moment, or from showing up for ten-minute meetings about a sticky problem to making a week-long commitment to inservice training. Actions like those were the visible signs that the faculty read as indicators of the principal's support of their efforts and interest in their work.

People we interviewed told us when their principals were helpful: The principal built trust with the total facutly. He served as a sounding board for the faculty. The principal ran interference for project staff with the central office. He was an advisor and helper if problems occurred. He recognized outstanding contributions of faculty members and gave them strokes. You always know where you stand with her. The principal gave personal support to the project director. He hosted social gatherings with project staff and members of the funding agency to give visibility to the project and to express thanks. She showed up at meetings when she was needed. The principal participated in inservices for teachers.

Other principals were not so helpful: The principal did not give overt support to the project. He would not explain the benefits of the project to the faculty. He gave the project permission to exist but did not support the people or goals. The principal did not participate in the inservice workshop. He acted bored when the project was discussed in meetings.

In successful projects, teachers described principals with words such as: liking, respect, trust, enthusiasm, promoter, advocate of goals, supportive, encouraging, positive, enthusiastic, and high energy. The principal's support and participation could take many forms, depending on the staff's capabilities and expectations. Most staffs appreciated signs of initiative on the part of the principal. Sometimes it was sufficient for the principal to let the staff know that he or she was available to help; that was especially true when the staff knew that the principal had confidence in them.

Teachers who were critical of their principals' support and participation used words like: lacks interpersonal skills to give support; is not perceptive; is not accessible; is minimally involved; acts bored and leaves meetings early; is too far removed; gives rational but not emotional support.

It appears that two things are important. The first is the principal's own feeling of commitment and priority put on the project; in some cases the staff never believed that the principal supported the project despite any actions that appeared to say he did. The second is the principal's ability to demonstrate support. Some principals were viewed as willing to support the project but unable to do so because of poor interpersonal skills or an inability to manage their time in a way that would free them to attend to the project.

The dilemma confronting the principal is the same one we identified in discussing role clarity, and it is the question of how much of the principal's limited time and energy can go to the project.

It is abundantly clear that the principal's demonstrated support is critical to the success of an externally funded project, which has the potential of being very stressful for a school. Putting new resources and people into the building upsets routines and relationships. Trying new behaviors can cause anxiety among teachers and also elicit criticism from the district office or community. The principal's social support and participation is his or her way of saying, "I'm in this thing with you, and I will be here to back you up when you need it."

Dwight D. Eisenhower neatly illustrated our point during a cabinet meeting. Pulling a piece of string out of his pocket, he

147

laid it on the table. Placing his finger at one end of it, he began to push the string to where he wanted it to go, naturally, the string simply crumpled up about itself. Moving his finger to the opposite end, he easily pulled the string where he wanted. People, Ike commented, can be pulled where you want them to go a lot easier than they can be pushed.

PROVIDING EVALUATION AND FEEDBACK

The final set of important behaviors by principals that we observed was their willingness and ability to provide feedback and evaluation to project staff and teachers who were experimenting with new behaviors. We did not hear many reports when this wasn't being done, but in some projects we heard comments like: The principal provided objective feedback to the staff on their work. He served as a sounding board for the project director and told him how he thought things were going. The head teacher gave feedback to teachers on how she felt things were going in the project. The principal got us to look at our own behavior and assess what we were doing.

Three kinds of actions seem to be important. The first is that the principal make an effort to get information: the principal is kept fully aware of the project by the coordinator; he developed monitoring and evaluation systems for the project; she always knows what is going on in classrooms. The second is giving that information to teachers and project staff so they have an independent assessment of their efforts: Pamela Bishop always says what she means; you know where you stand with her; the principal provides objective feedback to the staff. The final one is being quick to give encouraging information: "the principal recognizes teachers' outstanding contributions and gives them strokes."

In all, teachers and project staff seemed to appreciate receiving feedback about their behaviors and about the progress of their efforts from the school's central figure. The information itself was probably useful in helping them gain an independent assessment of their work, but it also was probably helpful as a signal from the principal that she or he was in-

148

terested in the project and found it important enough to make critical, objective judgments about it.

SUMMARY

We found that projects we studied had life cycles and that different behaviors of principals were important in each. In the planning and initiation stage, principals needed to be actively involved, to agree with the project's central concepts, to provide some input, and to communicate enthusiasm for the project to others. In the temporary system stage, principals were needed to acquire staff, space, and resources; to negotiate budget and expectations with the funding agency; to coordinate and link the project with the district office; and to create groups of staff and others to carry out the project or give it support. In the development and implementation stage, successful principals "moved backstage" and let staff take over, while continuing to provide support and assistance; the key seemed to be a sensitivity about what to do himself or herself and what to let others do. In the ending and institutionalization stage, the principal's key role was in deciding what would remain and in securing resources to continue parts of the project.

We identified eight kinds of behaviors as crucial. Four had to do with the tasks of the project: understanding the central concept of the project, commitment to the project's vision and concept, negotiating with competing environmental pressures, and using and allocating resources. Four were directed to building relationships and giving support: achieveing role clarity, encouraging involvement and participation, providing social support and active participation, and giving feedback and evaluation.

We did *not* discover the "magic wand" that principals can wave to make projects successful. No one leadership style, role, or behavior seemed to be uniformly successful or unsuccessful. Rather, we found that a variety of styles, role, and behaviors worked—or didn't work—depending on how well

149

they were fitted to the particular staff, project, school, and principal.

We *did* discover that the successful principal was one who could accurately diagnose his or her situation and adapt style and action as appropriate to the particular contingencies of that situation. In the next chapter we shall have a great deal to say about how principals can recognize those contingencies and about what tools are available to the principal in taking action that matches what is needed.

CHAPTER *4*

Managing Externally Funded Projects

In this chapter we present guidelines for managing extrnally funded projects, based on what we learned from the case studies, the literature on principals and change, and our own experience. We first describe the "Situational Leadership Theory" of Hersey and Blanchard. We then discuss the application of that model to choosing appropriate leadership styles. Next we present suggestions about skills that are necessary for effective project management. Finally, we discuss the particular actions appropriate to the four stages of a project's life.

The reader will not find a kit bag of techniques that always work. Instead we offer a contingency model of project leadership. We believe that taking effective action depends on having information about one's self, the staff and school, the system, and the project, and on having a repertoire of styles and roles so that appropriate action can be matched to the particular situation.

Situational Leadership Theory

The central idea in Hersey and Blanchard's contingency model is that effective leadership depends largely on the manager's knowledge of subordinates' and willingness and ability to assume responsibility. The principal engages in task-oriented behavior or relationship-oriented behavior, depending on what is needed. The level of behavior may be either

151

"high" or ' low." Thus, there are four ways to describe the principal's orientation at a given moment:

- *high task/low relationship:* the leader takes the initiative in defining goals, roles, and tasks; communication is mostly oneway, from leader to subordinate; the leader "tells" (to use Tannenbaum and Schmidt's term) the group what to do, or does it himself or herself;
- *high task/high relationship:* the leader exercises considerable initiative, but the activity is directed *both* at accomplishing tasks *and* at developing relationships and support;
- *low task/high relationship:* initiative is shared between leader and subordinate, with most of the leader's activity directed toward developing relationships with staff and among staff members;
- *low task/low relationship:* the leader delegates responsibility and authority, essentially letting subordinates run the show, while perhaps joining or supporting the group.

No style is automatically either "good" or "bad '; all are appropriate in some situations but inappropriate in others. Often, the principal will use them in the order listed. Here is how Martin Lawrence in Case 3 used the styles:

High task/low relationship.—Examining student test scores and listening to comments of parents and teachers, Lawrence unilaterally decided that the school had a problem and needed to do something about it.

High task/high relationship.—Involving parents and teachers, Lawrence worked with them to gain acceptance of the problem and to search for solutions. While he took an active role in preparation of the proposal, he also began to build the temporary system needd to carry out the project.

Low task/low relationship.—With the funding of the proposal, Lawrence's actions were directed mainly toward providing the support needed to implement ·it, including hiring staff, explaining to parents and staff why the project was a good idea, and building supportive relationships with district and funding agency personnel.

Low task/low relationship.—After the project was launched, Lawrence's direct involvement with it decreased dramatically as he relied on project staff to carry it out; he stood ready to aid in problem-solving and give support, but the initiative rested with others.

How does a principal know—as Lawrence and other successful principals seemed to know—when to take the initiative (a "high" level of behavior) and when to let others take it (a "low" level)? And how does a principal know when to attend mainly to "task" issues and when to deal mostly with "relationship" issues?

Recall that in discussing the cases in Chapters 2 and 3 we often used the words "energy," "ability," "commitment," and "readiness." We said that it seemed to take a certain amount of those resources to make a project go. Sometimes they were supplied by the principal and sometimes by others. At times principals had to create or discover them in the staff. (Unsuccessful projects, like Case 11, failed when nobody had energy for them, the staff was not ready to take on the project, no one was committed to making them work, or task and relationship abilities were lacking.)

Part of the answer, then, is that when the staff is not ready, willing, able, and energetic, it is up to the principal to supply or create those resources. When others *do* have them, the principal will do well to stand back and let others take the initiative.

The other part of the answer must come from the principal's ability to diagnose situations, to know whether task issues or relationship issues are paramount at that particular time. Achieving the project's objectives requires *both* that certain tasks be accomplished and that staff members' relationships are in good working order. At times the principal will find that progress depends on seeing that a particular job is done, while at other times he or she will see that the greater need is to provide social-emotional support to staff.

153

By what signs does the principal recognize the staff's level of ability and commitment to accomplish project tasks or to attend to their own working relationships? Hersey and Blanchard distinguish two dimensions: technical skill and knowledge needed for the task, and psychological factors such as confidence, commitment, and good working relationships.[1] That is, the principal must look for two kinds of indicators. The first consists of signs that staff members have task-skills to behave in new ways and relationship-skills to become an effective team. The second consists of signs that people believe there is a problem, feel committed to solving it, work well with each other and the principal, and so on.

We will be more specific about those indicators of readiness when we present our recommendations about project life cycles and principals' behaviors. Here are the general kinds of indicators we have in mind for the principal to use in deciding how much initiative to delegate to staff and how much to keep to themselves. This list is adapted from materials on decision management created by Consulting Exchange, a private consulting firm based in Eugene, Oregon, and Santa Cruz, California.

CHARACTERISTICS OF THE PRINCIPAL

1.1 *Position power.*—The extent to which the principal has the authority to make things happen by virtue of his or her position in the organization.

1.2 *Expertise.*—The knowledge, skills, and experience relevant to both task and relationship dimensions.

1.3 *Personal beliefs.*—One's beliefs and assumptions about

---

[1]Hersey and Blanchard use the term "maturity level" of the group in relation to the task, to the leader, and to themselves. They make it clear that "maturity" should be considered *"only in relation to a specific task to be performed"* (1977: 161) and should not be considered a global judgment about the group. Still, we think the term is unfortunate in that it can carry too many connotations of "irresponsible" or "childish" behavior when what is meant is an objective assessment of task and people skills, degrees of commitment, expectations of the leader, and the like. We therefore generally avoid using their term, preferring alternatives such as "readiness."

people, organizations, change, including expectations of staff and their ability to take responsibility.

1.4 *Confidence in staff.*—The principal's belief that staff can take responsibility, based on knowledge of their performance, principal-staff relations, and interpersonal relations among staff members.

CHARACTERISTICS OF THE STAFF

2.1 *Orientation to task and goal.*—Staff's attitude about the project, acceptance of the problem, commitment to its goals, and motivation to invest time and energy in the project.

2.2 *Expertise.*—The knowledge, skills, and experiences needed for the project; expertise includes both technical ability (instructional technique, familiarity with materials, etc.) and people ability (good communication, decision-making, and problem-solving skills, for example).

2.3 *Orientation to principal.*—Expectations about the appropriate leadership style and role for the principal, beliefs about the principal's expertise and values, etc.

2.4 *Staff relationships and norms.*—The quality of working and interpersonal relationships, clarity of roles, norms and "rules of the game," trust, and agreed-upon procedures of operation.

CHARACTERISTICS OF THE TASK

3.1 *Complexity.*—The scope of activities needed to complete the task, one's freedom to implement various solutions within constraints of the system, the location and accessibility of information needed, etc.

3.2 *Quality and acceptance requirements.*—The extent to which one solution clearly stands out as preferable to others (quality) and the extent to which a variety of solutions are acceptable but the important thing is people's commitment ot the solution (acceptance).

3.3 *Time.*—What deadlines for action must be met, who has time available for deciding or acting, etc.

155

To summarize our discussion thus far, the principal may direct her or his activity to "task" issues or to "relationship" issues (and sometimes both). Which set of issues to attend to depends, first, on what is needed to move the project forward and, second, whether the staff has the energy, ability, commitment and readiness—or whether they must be supplied or created by the principal. Generally the principal begins in a "high task/low relationship" style, then moves through "high task/high relationship" and "low task/high relationship" styles, and ends in a "low task/low relationship" style.

We can now combine the various elements, as represented in Figure 5. The principal's behavior changes as staff takes on more initative for tasks and relationships. Initially (Window 1—high task/low relationship) the principal takes the lead in defining the problem and beginning to develop the solution. As more people are involved (Window 2), the principal helps define tasks, goals, and roles for the project, but also attends to working relationships among members of the temporary system and school staff. Next (Window 3), staff members begin to implement the project, so the principal's attention shifts *from* the project's core tasks *to* maintaining effective working relationships and supporting the staff. Finally (Window 4), when the project is a routine part of the school, the principal does not have to exert special leadership for it beyond what is normally given to the school's operation.

There are similarities between the four parts of Hersey and Blanchard's model and the four stages of a project's life cycle. "Planning and initiation" is usually a "high task/low relationship" stage (especially at first) when the principal must initiate activities to get the project going. Building a temporary system is often a "high task/high relationship" stage in which the principal initiates tasks for the temporary system but also helps its members create smooth working relationships. In development and implementation, project staff and teachers work to create and put in place project activities, while the principal concentrates on supporting and facilitating roles; that makes it a "low task/high relationship" stage.

156

FIGURE 5

Situational Leadership Model for Managing Externally Funded Projects
Adapted from Paul Hersey and Kenneth H. Blanchard, *Management of Organizational Behavior*, 3rd Ed. (Englewood Cliffs, N.J.: Prentice-Hall, 1977).

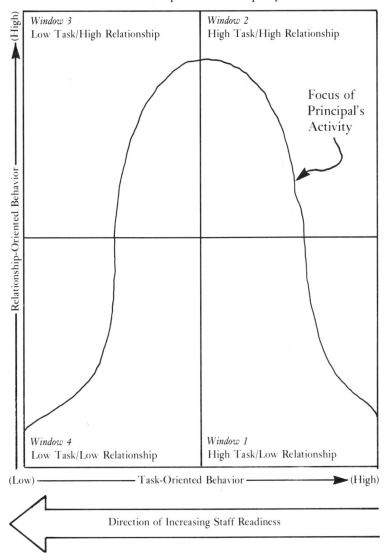

Effective Principal's Leadership Styles

The parallels should not be pushed too far, however. The staff's readiness will rise and fall as new situations call for new skills and commitments. Also, ending and institutionalization is usually a stage in which many problems and issues recur as principal and staff must find ways to operate without outside funding. The principal's task and relationship activity will usually increase accordingly.

The Hersey-Blanchard model helps us understand two patterns we found in successful projects. The first was the one in which the principal began as a "leader" and then moved backstage into a "manager" role. That is, the principal had to take a high-task role in defining the problem and finding the solution because staff did not recognize the problem, feel a commitment to solving it, or have the skills needed to secure funding.[2] In the second pattern, the principal did not have to supply the energy or direction because the problem was already owned by the staff and other people had ideas about its solution. In those cases the principal could initially attend to relationship issues, and even relinquish initiative for dealing with them in short order.

About Leadership Styles and Roles

By "leadership style" we mean the consistent pattern of behaviors and roles that principals use when working with others—*especially as perceived by those other people*. It is people's images of the principal's actions—rather than the principal's intentions—that determine their reactions and responses to the principal's behavior.[3]

[2]But "low relationship" never means "*no* relationship." Even when concentrating on the task dimension, the principal must keep in mind the effect of her or his actions on relationships and feelings among staff members. That is especially true in the early part of a project, when actions may have long-term consequences. Case 8, for instance, illustrates what happens when the principal focuses entirely on "task" and ingores "relationship": the principal assigned a convenient space to the project (task) but neglected to consult the teacher who was displaced (relationship). The result was hard feelings among the staff, feelings which were never entirely overcome. In sum, we do not mean attending entirely to one dimension and neglecting entirely the other; rather, it is a question of which dimension is emphasized over the other at any given time.

To repeat ourselves, *there is no one best leadership style that is appropriate for all situations.* What is appropriate and effective depends on the person, the situation, the task, and the expectations of subordinates. Ideally, the principal would have a repertoire of leadership styles, would be able to diagnose the situation, and would use the appropriate style. (That seemed to be true of Bill Foster in Case 5.)

There are, however, constraints on the principal's abilities to choose and carry out some leadership styles. Hersey and Blanchard (1977: 134) list as constraints the style and expectation of the leader, subordinates, superiors, associates, and the organization, as well as job demands. Some constraints are external, such as expectations of others and norms of the system. Others are internal, and include the principal's philosophy of management, conceptions of what the staff and system expect, and degree of comfort in using different kinds of power.

Even given those constraints, though, the principal does have freedom of choice. The principal can control those constraints that are self-imposed, while others (such as expectations of staff) can be changed through role negotiation.

IDENTIFYING LEADERSHIP STYLES

Most people we interviewed identified principals' leadership styles as "authoritarian," "democratic," or "laissez faire." We have not used those descriptions. We prefer the descriptions of leadership styles given by Tannenbaum and Schmidt (telling, selling, testing, consulting, delegating, and joining), and Hersey and Blanchard's four orientations: high task/low relationship, high task/high relationship, low task/high relationship, and low task/low relationship. Those two descriptive schemes direct our attention to task and relationship di-

[3]One always hopes, of course, that intention matches effect, but a moment's reflection makes us realize that there are many situations in which intentions are misinterpreted or misunderstood. In the case studies, several principals intended to demonstrate confidence in staff by delegating responsibility for the project, while faculty perceived that action as a signal of lessened interest and support.

mensions of leadership, to weighing quality and acceptance requirements, and to thinking about the particular factors important in choosing a style—task, situation, person, and group.

Each of the orientations described by Hersey and Blanchard is appropriate at some times and inappropriate at others; they may be perceived as effective or ineffective. When *high task/low relationship* is appropriate, the leader is seen as providing a well-defined structure for accomplishing tasks. When it is not, the leader may be seen as imposing goals or tasks on subordinates and being unconcerned about their preferences. When *high task/high relationship* is appropriate, the leader is perceived as attending to the group's needs for both structure of the tasks and support for their social-emotional needs. When it is not, group members may view the leader as "interfering," giving them more guidance than they want. *Low task/high relationship* is viewed as appropriate when group members feel the leader trusts their abilities and is genuinely concerned about working relationships. It is usually seen as inappropriate if the group feels that the leader is shirking responsibility or is interested only in being seen as a "good guy." Finally, when *low task/low relationship* is appropriate, the leader is seen as clearly delegating authority and responsibility to the group and as recognizing that they do not particularly need social-emotional support. When this style is not appropriate, the leader is seen as abdicating responsibility and ignoring group members' feelings.

CHOOSING A LEADERSHIP STYLE

Perhaps the two most important considerations in choosing a leadership style are how well the style matches personal preferences and how well the style matches expectations of the group.

One important factor is how well the various leadership styles match the principal's motivations, especially achievement, affiliation, and influence. All three motivations, however, do not provide equally effective bases for leadership.

Some research shows that principals who have high *achievement* needs often keep too much responsibility to themselves, can become bogged down in details of operation, and delegate too little responsiblity. Managers with high *affiliation* needs can be ineffective when they must make hard choices that may discomfort others; wanting to be liked, affiliative-oriented managers often shy away from those choices. Administrators with high *influence* needs can be very effective or very ineffective. If their style of influence is controlling and dominating others, they usually do not elicit more than minimum compliance from subordinates. If their style is one of involving others, finding responsibilities to match interests and capabilities, and generally "pulling" rather than "pushing" others, it can be a very productive style.

The difference between influence-oriented managers who think people must be dominated and those who think people can be encouraged is probably related to their differing conceptions of people. Douglas McGregor identified two conceptions of human nature as Theory X and Theory Y. Theory X is a "pessimistic" view of human nature which assumes that most people find work distasteful, are not ambitious or creative, and must be closely controlled and coerced to achieve organizational objectives. Theory Y is an "optimistic" view which assumes that people can be self-motivated, take pleasure in work, are creative, and want to take initiative and responsibility.

We personally find Theory Y the more comfortable one, because it matches our beliefs about people and our values about working relationships; however, everyone has encountered times when subordinates or colleagues must be pressured to accomplish work that needs to be done.

How can the principal learn which leadership style feels most comfortable to her or him? One way is to see if the styles we have presented describe the principal's preferences. Also, in *Management of Organizational Behavior* (1977), Hersey and Blanchard provide a self-scoring questionnaire to help managers identify their styles. Other instruments exist. Rensis

161

Likert (1967) developed a continuum of four leadership styles, based mainly on the amount of confidence managers have in subordinates. Dorothy Jongewood (1974) has applied the theory of Transactional Analysis to leadership styles. The Leader Behavior Description Questionnaire (Halpin, 1959) provides another description of leadership style. Other instruments are available in *The Second Handbook of Organization Development in Schools* (Schmuck, Runkel, Arends, and Arends, 1977).

The principal can take any of these self-administered tests to gain a perspective on leadership style. Another way of gathering that information is to ask faculty members, formally or informally, to describe the principal's leadership style and its effects on the school. (This may be a situation in which it is best to have a consultant or other outside person gather the information. People are more likely to be candid with a third party, especially if they are assured that their comments will not be individually identified. A consultant can also help the principal analyze the information and plan action based on it.)

ROLES OF THE PRINCIPAL

The principal will take on a variety of roles or functions during the course of the project. Some have to do primarily with providing task leadership—defining goals, linking the project with the system, etc. Others are mainly oriented to relationships—providing social-emotional support, clarifying expectations, etc. The first six of the following roles are taken by the principal in relation to the staff, while the final three are those taken in relation to the system and environment:

1. *Leader.*—Especially in early stages of the project, the principal probably needs to take the lead in defining the problem, generating enthusiasm for solving it, and finding resources to deal with the problem.

2. *Manager.*—Especially in the later stages of the project, the principal usually will "move backstage" to a less directive role, ready to provide on-the-spot problem-

solving and continued support of the project and its staff.

3. *Employer.*—The principal is a key person in hiring project staff or assigning (or enlisting) faculty to staff the project.

4. *Delegator.*—To develop staff ownership of the project, the principal will need to delegate authority and responsibility to the temporary system, providing clear guidelines as to the limits of their action.

5. *Supporter.*—Project and non-project staff will need attention, sympathy, encouraging words, and facilitative actions from the principal as they struggle through the rough parts of implementing the project.

6. *Information source.*—The principal has an "outside" perspective on the project and can provide objective feedback and evaluative information about how the project is affecting students, the school, and the system and environment.

7. *Advocate.*—The principal must speak articulately for the project to staff and to others, defending it against critics, and explaining its goals and benefits to a variety of audiences.

8. *Linker.*—The principal is the project's major link to important parts of the "outside world," including the central office, other staff members, the school board, and the community.

9. *Resource acquirer.*—The principal has the position power, mobility, contacts, and decision-making authority to acquire and allocate resources—tangible and intangible—for the project.

Taking on those roles depends on having skills to perform them and knowing when a given role is appropriate.

Skills for Project Management

We describe skills in managing projects under three general headings: personal awareness and abilities, interactions with staff, and dealing with the system.

163

We have said that the principal's support is crucial to a project, and our belief is amply supported by evidence from research, our own experience, and the cases reported in Chapter 2. It is also important that the principal communicate and demonstrate that commitment to others. Feeling a genuine commitment, communicating it to others, and taking effective action on behalf of the project rests, in turn, on self-awareness, conceptual abilities, and interpersonal communication skills that include advocacy and negotiation.

Self-awareness.—Commitment to a project probably depends on the principal's beliefs that it is good for children, appropriate to the school, and compatible with his or her own beliefs and values. Our suggestion is that the principal test her or his reaction to a project and measure the degree of commitment by answering questions such as these:

- Is this project really important to me? Why do I want it? What are the benefits for students, staff, school, and myself?
  - How does this project fit with my educational philosophy, values, and goals?
- Am I willing to change my behavior to make this project successful? What activities and tasks that now occupy my time am I willing to give up or reduce to devote time to the project? Where does it fit in my priorities for myself and the school?
- Will this project be worth the extra effort, uncertainty, anxiety, and upset of normal school routines that will inevitably happen?
- Am I willing to fight for this project in the face of misunderstanding or opposition from school board, central office, and community?

If the answers to those questions are positive—if the principal finds that the project is compatible with his or her beliefs and values, and seems to be worth expending effort and incurring criticism for—then it is probably worth proceeding with the effort. If the answers are negative, we question whether the enterprise should be attempted.

Understanding the project.—While it is impossible—and probably unnecessary—for the principal to be expert in all programs and projects in the school, people we interviewed felt that the principal should have enough knowledge of the project to explain it to others and to provide leadership for it.

Understanding the project means having a familiarity with its goals, activities, and intended outcomes; it also means having a sense of how the project fits the customary operation of the school. How the principal comes to understand the project depends on how he or she best learns new things, whether by reading, talking with others, or taking part in inservice activities to get a feel for strategies, materials, etc.

Conceptualizing the system.—Taking effective action on behalf of the project depends in part on how the principal conceptualizes her or his abilities to make things happen within the system. Sarason (1971: 134) points out that everyone in schools is aware that they are part of a complex arrangement of roles, purposes, and traditions that we call "the system." Somewhere, out there, "they" are making things happen[4] Most people regard "the system" mainly as something that gets in their way, and within which they have little of no power. Sarason notes that the image people have may be accurate or inaccurate; what counts is that they act on their image (or conception) of the system. Too often, principals and others *anticipate trouble in relation to the system:* "Too frequently, the individual's conception of the system serves as a basis for inaction and rigidity, or as a convenient target onto which one can direct blame for most anything. The principal illustrates this point as well or better than most anyone else in the system" (Sarason, 1971: 134).

We do not know how some principals come to see them-

[4]We know of some teachers and principals who refer to the district office as "Fort Fumble." In another distirct, the administration building is known as "the Puzzle Palace." Another central office, located at the crest of a small hill, is refered to as "the Big Bluff."

165

selves as powerless within the system while others see themselves as being able to "work the system" and as able to make
things happen. Some say, "I can't do it because 'they' won't let
me," while others say, "I'll do it until somebody tells me I
can't." We suggest that when principals anticipate trouble
from the system, they stop to ask themselves, "What is the
source of my information and belief?" Other good questions
are, "What would really happen if I went ahead and tried it?
What could they do?" Put another way, "What is the worst
that can happen? And can I plan for that by preparing things
so that 'the worst' is unlikely to happen or by having a fall-
back position in case it does?"

Interpersonal communication skills.—Training in skills of interpersonal communication was the inservice need most frequently mentioned by people we interviewed. Those skills are
fundamental to effective leadership and, indeed, to all human
relationships. We include here skills such as genuineness, directness, clarity, eliciting information from others, talking
about feelings as well as about ideas and things, and clarifying
expectations for the relationship. In our own experience, these
skills seem to be most essential:

- *Paraphrasing:* stating in your own words what you understood the other person to mean, so you know that
  your understanding is the same as theirs.
- *Describing one's own feelings:* conveying what your emotional state or reaction is by putting a name on the
  feeling, so that others know what effect they are having
  on you.
- *Describing the other's behavior:* being specific about what
  you are reacting to (an interruption, action taken without consulting you, etc.) so that the other has the same
  information you do about what elicits your reaction.
- *Checking your impressions:* testing your understanding of
  how the other is reacting or feeling by describing it and
  asking the other to verify or correct your impression.[5]

It is easy for humans to misunderstand one another. It is
especially easy for a faculty to hear the principal's enthusiasm

166

for a new idea as a criticism of what they are doing now. Communication skills are especially important in creating a common point of reference and information as a basis for action; in letting the staff know that the principal understands the hopes, concerns, and anxieties of the staff and takes them into account in decisions; and in providing a two-way flow of information for sensing and dealing with mutual problems.

Communicating concern and enthusiasm.—It is easier for people to commit themselves to a project when they see that it has captured the enthusiasm of the principal. Conveying that message comprises both verbal statements and also actions that demonstrate concern and enthusiasm. Each principal has his or her own way of signalling enthusiasm, and each faculty has its own set of indicators that it reads as signals about what the principal is thinking. In our view, the important thing is probably that there by a match between word and deed—that the principal's statements of support be translated into actions that make it clear that the principal is devoting time, attention, and energy to the project.

Advocacy.—The principal is called on to be an advocate for the project before a variety of audiences. Skillful advocacy begins with understanding what it is that people want to know, and what it is about the project that they may dislike. That means that the principal needs to know whether others object to the aims of the project and the definition of the problem that prompted this objection, or whether they object to the new ways in which teachers and students are behaving. People may also feel that other needs of higher priority are being neglected for the sake of the project. Skillful advocacy, further, requires the ability to understand things in others' frames of reference. It also includes skills of speaking clearly and articulating what is important and worthwhile about the

[5]These skills, ways of learning and practicing them, and their application are discussed in greater detail in Schmuck, Runkel, Arends, and Arends (1977). There is a vast literature on interpersonal communication skills, a large variety of ways of explaining them, and many training programs in how to acquire them. We need not replicate all that here.

167

project, and using communication skills—especially paraphrasing—to understand their concerns.

Negotiation.—Acquiring resources from the system, dealing with the funding agency, and clarifying expectations all require skills in negotiation. In our view, negotiation is the normal way to get things done in schools. People negotiate roles, rules, relationships, exchanging resources, gaining legitimacy, and a host of other issues. Hanson (in Runkel, Schmuck, Arends, and Francisco, 1979: 34) notes:

> The negotiations in schools are *informal rather than formal* and virtually everyone participates when their interests are involved. When a troublesome situation arises for an individual or group, they seek to spin a network of negotiation around it . . . The agreements made in the contested zone [are] usually temporary and fragile, subject to re-negotiation the next time the same issue surfaces.

Yet it is often not clear that negotiation is seen as an acceptable or appropriate behavior. (At least in contract negotiations the sides are definitely drawn, there are formal rules for conducting negotiations, the issues are somewhat clear, and it is regarded as a legitimate activity.) Many people are uncomfortable with the "horse-trading" that negotiations require, and it violates norms that the school system should be seen as a happy and cooperative community. But experienced administrators know that schools are in many ways clusters or coalitions of power bases and special interests, and that maintaining the school's stability comes only at the cost of constant bargaining and negotiation. Two examples of what we mean by negotiating were displayed by Joe Lyons (Case 1), who negotiated a procedure with the business office to simplify handling the project's money, and by Martin Lawrence (Case 3), who negotiated with central office administrators to permit him to conduct a national search for project staff, although that was not usually done in his district.

We encourage the principal to try to make negotiation a "win-win" situation, in which a solution will be beneficial both to the principal and to others. The essential skills of negotiation are those of knowing what one considers important and what one is willing to give up; knowing whom to negotiate with, how the system operates, and who controls what; and knowing when and where to negotiate. Being a competent negotiator requires that the principal be willing to take moderate risks, feel confident in his or her abilities, and feel that she or he is "instrumental" and can make things happen. Among the important process skills in negotiation are advocacy, interpersonal communication, and problem-solving.

Gathering and using information.—One of the themes of this chapter is that effective action depends on having accurate information about self, staff, and system. Sensing the need for the project is largely a matter of being receptive to different kinds of information. Getting projects funded depends on knowing what funds are available and how one gets them. Determining a staff's readiness to undertake a project requires knowing their abilities, preferences, and attitudes. Dealing with the system means knowing how it works and who controls important resources. And so on.

There are several ways to gather information, both formal and informal. Generally, they fall into two categories: those that use paper and those that do not.

Using paper-and-pencil instruments is a quick way to get information from a lot of people. This category includes surveys and questionnaires, tests, and records.

- *Surveys and questionnaires* can be used to gather many kinds of information, from characteristics of people to their perceptions and opinions about school climate, student learning problems, and other topics. While questionnaires are quick and economical when one is dealing with a large number of people, compiling results is also time consuming, answers may be superficial, and sometimes the right questions may not be asked.
- *Student tests* provide data about student achievement, attitude toward school, etc., and the results can be used to identify learning problems and other concerns. Standardized (nationally normed) tests are usually statisti-

169

cally valid, but interpretation of their importance can be confusing, and they may not be relevant to the school's particular concerns. "Homegrown" tests are more relevant to one's individual concerns, but they are time consuming to create and may not be valid or reliable.

- *Records* give objective data on concerns such as attendance, discipline referrals, and the like. Their usefulness, though, depends on whether they contain the information one wants, and how well the recordkeepers keep records.

Information-gathering methods that do not rely on paper include interviews, informal conversations, observations, and group discussions.

- *Interviews* with structured questions can be used for several purposes, especially for learning peoples' perceptions and feelings about matters. The quality of the information depends largely on the rapport between the persons involved, and they are very time consuming.
- *Observations* can be of individuals, groups, or things. Classroom observations during teacher evaluations can yield information about classroom climate, discipline problems, and so on. Watching children on the playground reveals much about school climate. Walking down the halls gives good information about how people feel about being in the school. The usefulness of observations depends largely on how well the observer can find patterns in what she or he sees, and whether people being observed are "natural" in their behavior.
- *Conversations* in which professional or personal information is exchanged can reveal patterns that signal a problem. That happens, for instance, when several people approach the principal with a similar complaint. Using information from those informal contacts depends on the principal's skill in finding patterns and in testing impressions to make sure that complaints or problems are, in fact, widespread.
- *Group discussions*, as in faculty meetings, can be an eco-

nomical way to gather perceptions and opinions from people. Whether the information is accurate and useful depends on the skill of the meeting convener in leading the discussion, how much investment people have in attending to the topic of discussion, and whether people have enough trust in the principal and each other to share valid and important information about themselves.

Then there is the "grapevine." Almost every school has one. They're often extremely useful and informative, provided that people in them have access to accurate information and communicate it accurately. The trick is to get independent confirmation of information that comes through the grapevine.

Especially in acquiring information from parts of the system outside the school, whom you know is more important than what you know. Getting information outside the school means being hooked into the various formal and information communication networks that web the district, knowing who the accurate information sources and opinion leaders are, and cultivating the relationships that provide access to information.

Deciding which method of gathering information to use depends on several factors. The first is how important the information is: when the goal, issue, or problem at stake is vital, then acquiring information about it is worth the time and effort it takes. The second is the quality of the information: the principal needs to consider how likely it is that the information source and method will yield accurate and important information. The third is feasibility: sometimes getting the information simply isn't worth the cost (as, for example, in having teachers take two hours to fill our a questionnaire). The final one is the principal's estimate of whether the act of getting the information will create unnecessary antagonism (remember the two-hour questionnaire).

SKILLS FOR INTERACTING WITH STAFF

While all the abilities just listed are important for interacting with staff, here we call attention to four that are particularly important: involving others, giving support and feedback, clarifying expectations, and problem-solving.

Involving others.—Why should people want to become involved in projects? Partly because it appeals to some basic motives (see the discussion of these motives in Schmuck, Runkel, Arends, and Arends, 1977): feelings of *achievement* when the job is well done and students benefit; feelings of *affiliation* when teachers can escape some of the loneliness of teaching and work with valued colleagues; and feelings of *influence* when people feel they can gain greater control over what happens to them and the students for whom they are responsible. People want to become involved for other reasons. Sometimes they feel that involvement is a part of their job or position. Sometimes it is because they will be affected by the outcome and want to have a say in what happens. At other times, people may feel they represent a group whose interests must be protected. Others feel that they have expertise that would be useful in the project.

In addition to personal motivation, we think there are other conditions of readiness that influence whether a staff is prepared to undertake a project. Some recent research (Runkel, Schmuck, Arends, and Francisco, 1979) indicates that conditions such as these should be in place before major changes are attempted. The conditions we discuss here are described in greater detail in Bell, Wyant, and Schmuck, *Diagnosing A Schools's Readiness for Change* (1979).

- *Internal press for change:* how many people in the school are unhappy with the present situation, feel that the proposed project is a solution to the problem they feel, believe that improvement is possible, and think that the project's benefits will outweigh its costs?
- *Stability of staff:* how many people now at the school plan to stay, so that those who initiate the project will be around to carry it out; how many people believe the principal will stay in her or his position long enough to see the project through; what other changes are being tried, changes which use energy that might go to the

project; and how many other groups, meetings, committees, departments, and other involvements claim a share of the faculty's attention and energy?

- *Skill in collaborative group work:* what is the extent of relationships skills among the staff, including abilities to communicate accurately, come to decisions that are clear and supported, conduct meetings that are worth people's time, and work with diverse philosophies and values?

- *Norms supporting collaborative work:* do the implicit rules about "the way we do things here" encourage collaboration, communication even in conflictful or emotionally charged situations, perseverance at group tasks in spite of frustrations, expression of feelings, and using third-party helpers in conflicts and difficulties?

- *Spirit of risk-taking:* to what extent are people willing to take on extra work on behalf of the school even though trying the new behaviors may be uncomfortable; are they willing to take inservice training; what other kinds of stress are they experiencing that may interfere with their ability to devote energy to the project?

We do not know what proportion of those indicators must be favorable to augur success for a project; there probably is no magic number. We do know, however, that success is more likely when favorable conditions are a substantial proportion of the whole.

Involving others means influencing them to change their behavior from customary or routine ways and to act in new ways to create and implement the project. Roger Harrison (1976) describes four influence styles that can be used to involve people: reward and punishment, participation and trust, common vision, and assertive persuasion.

The use of *reward and punishment* involves giving pressures and incentives. It includes evaluating others and rewarding or punishing them according to how well they meet one's requirements. The second aspect of it is prescribing goals and expectations, setting clear standards about how others' per-

173

formance will be judged. Finally, applying incentives and pressures is used to secure compliance. This style can be effective only when one controls rewards that others want, especially tangible or intangible resources. The use of reward and punishment can often provoke a counter-reaction and is usually effective only so long as one can monitor the performance of others.

While reward and punishment is a "hard" style, *participation and trust* is a "soft" style (pulling rather than pushing). It involves, first, personal disclosure, and an open acceptance of limits on one's knowledge and resources. It also includes recognizing and involving others by drawing out their contributions and listening to them, giving credit for their suggestions, and delegating responsibility to them. Finally, it involves testing and expressing understanding, especially by paraphrasing others' statements. Participation and trust can be an effective style when a high-quality solution depends on pooled resources, when the others' commitments to carrying out actions independently are important, and when others have knowledge and resources that one does not have. It does, though, tend to be ineffective when speed and action are more important than quality of a decision or action, when the principal has all the expertise needed to act and others do not, and when others perceive that it is not in their best interests to cooperate.

The style of *common vision* is the one often associated with charismatic leaders. It aims at identifying a common vision of the future and strengthening people's belief that the vision can become a reality through their collective effort. It appeals to others' emotions and values, activating their commitment toward personal goals and channelling their energy toward a common purpose. The two components are articulating exciting possibilities—getting others to "dream" about what they might do—and generating a shared identity by helping them feel the strength that comes from being part of a unified group. Common vision is effective when the leader is liked and respected, when people are experiencing problems but are not

174

sure how to solve them, and when what is done is less important than acceptance of the challenge. It does not work when the principal is mistrusted by staff and it can backfire when hopes are raised but then are not fulfilled.

The style of *assertive persuasion* involves the use of facts, logic, and ideas to convince others, so that the basis of agreement is the soundness of the principal's arguments. It is based on logical arguments and reasoning for and against positions. It can be effective when one has high prestige or credibility with another; when the other trusts the principal's motives for trying to exert influence; when the other perceives his or her interests as similar to the principal's; and when the principal is the only readily available source of information. It is not likely to be effective when some condition disposes others to be distrustful of the principal, when others hold very strong opinions about the matter, or when there is already some conflict in the relationship.

We do not wholeheartedly endorse or reject any of these approaches; probably every attempt by principals to encourage faculty to support and become involved in a project rests on several of these styles.[6] Implementing the project will require that staff members act with a great deal of independence as they try new behaviors in the classroom, since they need to be self-motivated. Self-motivation among staff is more likely if the principal uses the "soft" styles, although using those styles does require a fairly high degree of readiness and commitment as we have described them.

Finally, successfully involving others usually depends on some degree of trust between faculty and staff. Trust is built when staff approve of the principal's values, feel comfortable with her or his leadership style, and believe that she or he will look out for their interests in making decisions. The best way to create trust is to build a good track record of sensitivity to the staff and their needs and interests, of supporting them

---

[6]For a good discussion of how administrators try to enlist cooperation of teachers—and how teachers can resist those efforts—see Wolcott (1977).

when they need it, and of being dependable in carrying out the tasks of the principalship.

One thing that should be clear from this and other discussions is that creating conditions receptive to undertaking projects is usually something that happens over a fairly long period of time. Where relations between staff and principal are strained and distrustful, it is unlikely that staff will enthusiastically give extra time and effort to a project at the principal's request. Where working relationships between principal and staff are in good order already, faculty members are much more likely to respond to the principal's enthusiasm for the new undertaking.

Proving support and feedback.—The set of behaviors most often mentioned by staff as crucial to a project's success was the principal's social support of staff involved in the project. Providing objective information and feedback was also often mentioned as an important behavior.

People need to know that their efforts on behalf of the project are recognized and appreciated, just as they need objective information on how they're doing in their attempts to implement the project. The principal can give support in many ways.

Giving support means giving words of encouragement, reinforcements, "strokes," and expressions of thanks. Those words can be given in informal conversations, as notes in the teacher's mailbox, as mentions in the staff bulletin, or in whatever way the principal customarily does it. Support also means giving visibility and credibility to the project and staff; doing so involves demonstrations of the principal's personal commitment to the project, his seeing that the project has appropriate space and adequate supplies, his accessibility to the project staff, and his willingness to go to bat for the project by advocating it with central office superiors and by defending it from undue criticism. People we interviewed told us that those actions were important; they also valued the principal's willingness to take on odd jobs—Joe Lyons in Case 1 was "bus driver and tour guide, tent-pole setter and camp cook."

The effectiveness with which feedback and evaluative information can be given to staff depends upon several things. First, there must be an agreement between principal and staff that giving feedback is part of the principal's role. It also helps to have staff and principal collaboratively decide what information is desired and how the feedback will be given. Finally, skill is required to convene meetings at which the feedback is discussed, its implications are considered, and the data provided by feedback are used by staff and principal to make decisions about altering action.[7]

Clarifying expectations.—Work in schools proceeds largely on the basis of a series of unwritten agreements and implicit understandings about who is expected to do what, as well as what kinds of behavior are required, permitted, or prohibited. When the school undertakes something out of the ordinary— such as an externally funded project—that involves behaviors that are not customary, it is time to make those agreements and understandings explicit. Doing so requires that the principal think through her or his expectations and then state them publicly. Project staff and others involved should have a similar opportunity to make their expectations explicit. Since new agreements will be called for as new stituations arise, principal and staff should be prepared to review and revise the expectations periodically.[8]

Problem-solving.—Many times principals in our study were called on to give on-the-spot problem-solving help when conflicts or concerns arose. The first step in effective problem-solving is figuring out what the problem is, and that requires converting frustrations into problems. Many things are frustrating, but they are not solvable problems until we can put a definite shape on them: "We will use the word *problem* to mean a discrepancy between a present state of affairs and a preferred

[7]For guidelines to gathering information, reporting it, and acting on it, see Schmuck, Runkel, Arends, and Arends (1977).

[8]Making expectations explicit can be stressful, since it is not customarily done, and since doing so involves a certain amount of risk and self-disclosure. Making effective agreements depends on interpersonal communication skills, a climate of trust, and some of the other conditions of readiness we discussed under "involving others."

state of affairs—sufficiently more preferred that one is ready to spend some energy to get there. Without the two parts—the current situation and the more desirable one—a problem has not been specified" (Runkel, Schmuck, Arends, and Francisco, 1979: 10). We distinguish three dimensions of problems as we define them:

- *Situation:* Is information needed that helps people understand what the situation is now?
- *Target:* Is information needed that clarifies the purpose or intent of the action?
- *Proposal:* Is information needed that helps develop alternative ways of solving the problem, evaluating their consequences, and selecting the most appropriate solution?

When the principal has the information and expertise needed to solve the problem, "telling" or "selling" styles may be appropriate. When that is not the case, collaborative problem-solving that involves "consulting" or "joining" may be called for. One consideration in selecting the appropriate style is which dimension of the solution is more important. N. R. F. Maier (1970) distinguishes two dimensions: the first is *quality*—whether one solution is clearly preferable to others; and the second is *acceptance*—when a variety of solutions can work but the key is whether the persons affected can support the solution.

Problem-solving is often carried out in formal or informal meetings, as is much of the work of the project in general. Effective meetings require a skillful convener, or meeting leader, who can lead the group in setting an agenda, clarifying action needed on each item, seeing that decisions are clear and accepted, and making sure that assignments for follow-up are made and accepted. The leader must help the group attend to process issues such as encouraging participation, resolving differences, expressing feelings, and maintaining good working relationships.[9]

[9]The principal can find many useful suggestions on ways to solve problems, make decisions, conduct effective meetings, and set goals in Schmuck, Runkel, Arends, and Arends, *The Second Handbook of Organization Development in Schools* (1977).

The many people who press their beliefs, values, and complaints on the schools inevitably knock at the principal's door. Further, it is usually the principal who must deal with the various regulatory agencies that demand reports or compliance with rules. And most every individual or group that is affected by the project—staff, parents, community, funding agency, central office, school board, students, and others—will have a different conception of the project and will act in sometimes conflicting ways on that conception. Finally, implementing the project will take a variety of tangible and intangible resources that are controlled by people in the school system or its environment. By environment we mean formal and informal groups in the community, as well as the funding agency and other bodies which are "outside" the school system but which have an effect on it. Inevitably, it falls to the principal to deal with those persons or groups.

Acquiring resources.—Staff members will need resources to implement the project that are not or cannot be supplied by the funding agency. That includes tangible resources, such as goods, services, and money, and intangible resources, such as approval, legitimacy, and information. The principal is in the best position to acquire resources, since she or he has more mobility, information about who controls the resources and access to them, and decision-making authority to acquire and allocate resources than other staff members.

The ability to acquire resources rests in large part on some of the personal abilities of the principal we discussed earlier, particularly conceptualization of the system and the principal's ability to influence it, interpersonal communication and negotiation skills, and gathering and using information.

The pieces of information needed are these: First, what tangible and intangible resources does the project need? Second, who controls those resources or knows where they are located? Sometimes that means knowing who is officially in charge of the resources, and sometimes it means knowing who

179

is the person—a clerk, secretary, or assistant, perhaps—who *really* knows how to expedite their delivery. Third, the principal should know what the system's formal and informal procedures for allocating resources are. If those procedures are helpful, then use them. If they serve mainly to block action, then some way around them must be found. (Joe Lyons in Case 1 worked with the district's business manager to find a way to use the school's petty cash fund to simplify spending money for the project, and Martin Lawrence in Case 3 convinced the personnel administrator to let him conduct a national search for project staff, although that was an unusual procedure in that district.)

Among the resources most important to the project are intangible ones, especially approval and legitimacy. One finding of the Rand studies (Greenwood, Mann, and McLaughlin, 1975) was that strong administrative support for all levels of the system appeared to be essential to successful project implementation. (The project in Case 10—with a town in decline and a succession of superintendents—was obviously in trouble in part because of the lack of support from the district's top administrators.)

In every district there are key decision-makers and opinion leaders, both formal and informal, without whose support innovations are unlikely to succeed.[10] Part of the principal's function is to secure political support from those persons and groups. Typically, important persons and groups include: central office administrators who have authority over the principal, curriculum specialists and other staff persons whose area of expertise or responsibility is affected by the project, colleagues and principals of other buildings who are in competition for the district's resources and who have norms about how principals are supposed to behave, members of the school board and groups whose interests they represent, community

[10]We know of one small district in which the way to get things done is to take the superintendent's wife to lunch, since she has considerable influence on his thinking and decisions.

180

agencies,[11] parent groups such as the school's advisory council, students, staff and community members of other externally funded projects, and so on. The principal can probably add to that list.

Securing approval from those groups depends on having accurate information about them and their concerns and preferences. With information, the principal can estimate the probable degree of support or opposition that can be expected from them. Particularly important is knowledge about people potentially in opposition. What is the nature of their concerns? Are they in disagreement with the aims of the project, do they disagree with the way it is carried out, or do they believe that other, higher priorities are being neglected for the sake of the project?

Perhaps the best way to acquire support from others is to find ways in which the project can help solve problems that they experience. That can involve the influence style we called "common vision"—creating shared goals so that others see that the project helps them achieve their objectives. Where that is not possible, the principal may need to fall back on "assertive persuasion" or even negotiating trade-offs and exchanges of resources or support.

Another important ingredient in securing support is being able to demonstrate that the project has the endorsement of all important parts of the school community. A parent or student who speaks enthusiastically and knowledgeably about the project at a school board meeting, for instance, can have a powerful effect. So can formal motions of endorsement from school advisory councils, parent organizations, the staff, and students.

Negotiating environmental pressures.—By "negotiating" we mean both "making one's way through" (as, for example, an obstacle course) and what happens when teachers and the school board bargain about salaries. Schools exist in highly political and often capricious environments, and many people

[11]Teacher Corps Youth Advocacy projects such as ours, for example, involve agencies from the juvenile corrections system.

181

and groups want influence over what happens in schools. In many ways, the principal's most important interactions are with those environmental groups (and those within the system) rather than those with the teachers and students directly involved in the project.

Persons and groups have different perspectives on the project, because they have partial information, diverse values and beliefs, and conceptions of the way in which the project will affect them. It is a difficult task indeed to reconcile all those viewpoints, and the reconciliation is never complete or permanent. Even with complete information, some people may find themselves still opposed to the philosophy or strategy of the project. Understandings are always incomplete. New perceptions will arise as new situations arise and as people act on their understandings in the belief that others agree with them.

The funding agency is a key part of the project's environment, since it controls the resources that support the project. Funding agencies support projects which meet their goals, and those goals may not be the same as the school's. Often, funding agencies want to "use" the school as a test site for the development of a promising practice that can be disseminated, while the school may be mainly interested in acquiring services to help deal with immediate problems. And there are always strings attached to grant money in the form of reports, evaluations, and restrictions on the use of the money. Differences in goals and expectations can be the subject of intense and emotional negotiations between the funding agency and the project. We expect that most experienced principals and project staff are familiar with that process.

Strategies for negotiating environmental pressures are quite similar to those for acquiring communication, advocacy, and negotiation. It is in acquiring resources and negotiating environmental pressures that the principal takes on the roles we described as "advocate," "linker," and "resource acquirer."

We have described three sets of skills as valuable in managing externally funded projects. Personal awareness and abilities include self-awareness (clarity about one's own goals

182

and values), understanding the project, conceptualizing the system, interpersonal communication skills such as conveying concern and enthusiasm, advocacy, negotiation, and gathering and using information. Skills for interacting with staff include involving others, providing feedback and support, clarifying expectations, and problem-solving. Skills for dealing with the system are those of acquiring resources and negotiating competing environmental pressures.

We now turn to the four stages in the life cycle of a project and what behaviors of the principal are most helpful in each. For each stage, we identify the issues that are important and information the principal needs for effective action; the leadership styles, roles, and skills most appropriate; and those behaviors that people we interviewed said were essential to the success of their project.

Stage One: Planning and Initiation

This stage encompasses the steps from recognizing the need for a project to submitting a proposal for funding and adopting the project. The key tasks are defining the need, creating a shared awareness of the problem, locating funding sources, and preparing a proposal. Other tasks include involving faculty in defining the problem and creating the solution, and linking the staff with the funding agency.

THE PRINCIPAL AND LAUNCHING THE PROJECT

A central message of this book is that the principal's support is crucial to the success of externally funded projects. There are good reasons why the principal's commitment is so important. Without that commitment it is unlikely that the principal will devote the time, energy, and enthusiasm that the project needs to succeed, especially when she or he must endure criticism of the project. Further, the principal gives cues to the faculty about what is important and what kinds of effort will be rewarded or punished; school staffs are especially sensitive to those kinds of messages as indicators of where they should put their energy.

The principal's commitment must be more than verbal.

183

Earlier we introduced the distinction between "espoused theory" and "theory-in-practice," and we saw in Cases 8 and 11 what happens when teachers believe that the principal's statements of support are not backed by action or when the principal "allows but doesn't support" the project.

Two things are important: The first is the principal's own feelings about the project and her or his sense of how important the project really is. The second is how that commitment is communicated to others. We suggest that principals test their commitment by answering the questions we asked in the section entitled "Personal Awarness and Abilities." The principal also needs a working knowledge of the project, its goals and strategies, and how it will fit in with the faculty's beliefs and values and customary ways of doing things. The principal also should think ahead to what role she or he will play in the project; we will discuss that issue at length in the section on building a temporary system.

INTERACTING WITH THE FACULTY

In the cases in Chapter 2, we saw two ways in which projects were initiated. Sometimes, the principal recognized a problem, convinced others of its importance, and led the effort to secure funding to solve it. In other cases, the principal became aware that a project made available to the school would solve a problem the staff was experiencing. What actions are appropriate for the principal depend in part on which of those two ways a project gets going. In either case, launching the project is usually a "high task/low relationship" stage: the principal takes the initiative to bring the problem or solution to the faculty's attention. The orientation is toward defining problems, goals, and tasks rather than nurturing relationships.

As to leadership styles, *telling* and *selling* are high-risk strategies. Some principals who have a great deal of enthusiasm and very clear ideas about the problem and solution may be able to "tell" or "sell" the project to the faculty. We think that is unlikely unless the staff already has a great deal of

184

ownership in the problem, considerable trust in the principal's decisions, and the implicit or explicit agreement that it is appropriate for the principal to make commitments for the faculty withhout consulting them.

Testing and *consulting* are probably more appropriate strategies for most faculties. Testing says, "Here is my definition of the problem and my idea for solving it. What do you think of the idea?" Consulting involves defining the problem and then soliciting suggestions from the faculty for ways to solve it. Testing is more appropriate when the principal has learned of a project and wants the staff to consider adopting it; consulting is more appropriate when the principal senses a problem and wants to have the faculty consider creating a project to solve it.

It is unlikely that *delegating* or *joining* would produce results unless some group in the school had already defined the problem and was already searching for solutions.

There are several ways to sense that a problem exists, including students' scores on standardized tests, comments of teachers and others, and other signals that all is not right at the school. Opinion surveys, needs assessment instruments, school climate surveys, or indicators such as increases in discipline referrals or a large number of children with similar learning or social problems can also signal the existence of a problem. What is important is that the principal be receptive to those kinds of information or takes the lead in gathering information that reveals problems. The principal (usually in consultation with the staff) should be able to define the problem, conceive a more desirable situation, and believe that the problem is important enough to merit action. Further, the principal should have a good sense that the proposed solution or project are compatible with those of the existing staff and that the costs of upsetting the school's customary relationships and routines would be worth it.

We encourage principals to involve their faculties as soon as possible in discussions and decisions about the nature of problems and possible solutions. For one thing, those dis-

185

cussions can give the principal a great deal of information about the staff's readiness to undertake the project. Further, the staff's endorsement is crucial to securing outside funding and support from within the system. Finally, teachers will be asked to behave in new ways for the project, and they are more likely to commit themselves to sustaining the new behaviors if they have a hand in defining the problem and designing the solution.

Teachers we interviewed said three actions by the principal were particularly important in securing their commitment. The first was conveying his or her own enthusiasm for the project by speaking about it positively. The second was orienting faculty to the project, by explaining its benefits, clarifying its goals, and convincing them of the importance of the problem. The third was involving faculty in decisions about the project at an early stage, providing incentives for participation, and helping them develop an ownership in it. Those actions seem to us to reflect the influence styles we earlier identified as "common vision," "participation and trust," and a touch of "assertive persuasion."

DEALING WITH THE SYSTEM AND ENVIRONMENT

The two important tasks here are securing funding and gaining initial approval from key decision-makers in the system. There are many ways to get money to fund projects. For schools, the most likely sources are state or federal grants such as Title IV-C, career education, special education, other special interest agencies, teacher incentive programs, and so on. Many districts have persons whose job it is to find grant money, while information may also be available from country, regional, or state educational agencies or professional associations. Recently, the federal network of state facilitators has been formed to help link people who have educational needs with projects.

Writing proposals and "grantmanship" have become fairly sophisticated skills. The requirements of the many funding agencies are so diverse that there is little benefit in trying to provide a formula here. One source[12] lists as "basic principles" of proposal-writing:

1. The proposal should be neat, clean, and easy to read.
2. Write your proposal in English (not bureaucratese or, worse, education-language).
3. Make it brief.
4. Be positive.
5. Avoid unsupported assumptions.

In general, funding agencies will ask for these kinds of information:

- *Statement of problem:* what it is you're trying to solve.
- *Goals:* what it is you hope to do, and who you're doing it for.
- *Methods:* how you're going to solve the problem and reach the goals.
- *Evaluation:* how you will know whether you're succeeding.
- *Budget:* how much money you want, and what you want it for.
- *Support:* whether key people in the system endorse your effort, and whether the system will put in money to assist the project and continue it when external funding ends.
- *Utility:* whether the project has the potential for being helpful to others and can be disseminated.

When dealing with a particular funding agency and its requirements and format, the first rule is "follow instructions," the second rule is "follow instructions," and the third rule is "follow instructions."

We have already discussed the issues involved in securing support from key decision-makers. Major requirements are probably demonstrating the need for the project, the feasibil-

[12]Norton J. Kiritz, "Program Planning and Proposal Writing," *The Grantsmanship Center News*, May/June 1979. Reprints are available from the Grantsmanship Center, 1031 South Grand Avenue, Los Angeles, California 90015. Another source is Mary Hall, *Developing Skills in Proposal Writing* (2nd Ed.). It is available from Continuing Education Publications, P.O. Box 1491, Portland, Oregon 97207.

ity of doing it, and the school community's support for it, as well as how the project supports major goals and values of the system and essential parts of its environment.

Teachers and others we interviewed said that important actions of the principal in launching the project included writing the proposal or supervising its preparation, negotiating with the funding agency about budget and expectations, and convincing central office administrators, colleagues, and parents of the project's importance. One principal convinced the district to give funds to support a team of teachers to write the proposal during the summer. Those are all actions aimed at accomplishing tasks or providing structure and direction for others to accomplish them, confirming our view that planning and initiation is a "high task/low relationship" stage. Task considerations remain important while relationship issues increase in importance when the temporary system is formed to carry out the project.

Stage Two: Building a Temporary System

This stage involves bringing together the people and the resources to convert the ideas and promises in the proposal into concrete actions that implement the project. It may involve hiring staff or redefining some current members' roles. The key issues and tasks are locating the right people for the project staff, clarifying the principal's role in relation to them, defining their goals and roles, and integrating the temporary system with the rest of the school. It is a "high task/high relationship" stage for the principal. A great deal of task activity must be devoted to starting the temporary system on its job. The principal will also need to help create good working relationships and clear agreements among temporary system members and between them and other parts of the school and system.

Recall Miles's (1964: Chapter 19) discussion of the tasks that members of temporary systems face:

1. role definitions and clear expectations about how members will work together;

2. clear norms about appropriate behavior;
3. the potential for frustration due to too-high expectations and unrealistic goals;
4. acquiring the technical skills needed for the project and the people (relationship) skills needed to become an effective working group;
5. the potential for feelings of isolation and alienation from the regular faculty and school routine;
6. communication channels within the group and between it and other parts of the school and system;
7. linkages between the temporary and permanent systems so that teachers can use the outcomes of the group's efforts.

CLARIFYING THE PRINCIPAL'S ROLE IN THE PROJECT

Successful cases were those in which the principal and others had clearly defined roles to play, and in which the principal and others agreed on his or her role. Staff members knew what to expect from the principal, who had achieved a balance between the demands of the project and the demands of other administrative tasks. The two essential components were *clairty* so that role expectations were understood by all, and *agreement* so that both principal and staff expected the same thing.

The first step is for the principal to identify in his or her own mind what degree of participation in the project is desired, given other demands on time, energy, and attention. And that is a matter of setting personal priorities.

Selecting which role to take in the project depends on several considerations. One is the principal's own preferences. Another is consideration of constraints, both formal and informal, that limit the roles the principal can choose. A third is the principal's estimate of the costs and benefits of various roles. Another is expectations of staff that have been created by the history of interaction between principal and staff. A final one is the principal's consideration of strengths and weaknesses of members of the staff and temporary system. If

189

members of the project staff are strong in the technical skills of the project but do not have the relationship skills to become an effective working team, the principal may need to help them attend to developing communication channels, social-emotional support, decision-making procedures, and working agreements.

Here is one procedure for clarifying the principal's role. It involves defining expectations by both principal and staff, and then negotiating differences.

1. *Clarifying one's own expectations.*—Deciding what role one wants to take is a matter of listing those things that one feels are appropriate to one's position. Job descriptions usually are vague and inadequate, but they may be a place to start in listing expectations. The principal may also want to indicate what proportion of his or her time is available to the project.

2. *Soliciting information.*—The principal can also ask project and non-project staff to list their expectations for the principal's role. One possibility is for the staff to indicate their preferences for how they want to use the proportion of the principal's time available to the project.

3. *Comparing expectations.*—The principal's and staff's lists can be compared, noting points of agreement and disagreement. Where there are disagreements, the differences can be resolved through problem-solving or negotiation. As we noted, clarifying and negotiating expectations can be stressful, since it opens the principal up to more two-way influence than is usually the case in schools. We think the rewards in both effectiveness of action based on clear agreements and avoiding hard feelings that come from misunderstandings are worth it. Teachers we interviewed said it was helpful when principals clarified the other demands on their time that interfered with their participation in the project, and when they clarified their own role as well as others'.

Staffing the temporary system.—When hiring project staff members, or selecting them from among present faculty, we think the principal should look for three sorts of qualities: ability, motivation, and representation.

Ability means, first, technical skills to implement the project; that may include teaching skill, expertise in the content area, familiarity with materials, etc. It also means abilities in creating and maintaining smooth interpersonal relationships within the team and between it and the faculty.

By motivation we mean people's feeling of ownership of the problem and their commitment to expending the energy to solve it. Runkel, Schmuck, Arends, and Franciso (1979: 21) suggest that the principal look for persons with time and energy to devote to the project; those who have not succumbed to pessimism and cynicism; those who can be motivated by a vision of joint achievement, of greater control over their own work, and of closer interaction with colleagues; those who know that the new effort will require extra and sustained energy; those willing to learn new skills; and those who have some understanding of the complexity of the system within which they must operate and of the change process itself.[13]

The third consideration is representation. Members of the faculty must have some belief that the temporary system's members are "one of us" or in some way will represent and protect their interests. In some cases that means assuring representation from different grade levels or academic departments, while in other cases it may mean getting participants from different interest groups, points of view, or educational philosophies. In some cases, it may be wise to include appropriate district personnel—such as a curriculum specialist—in a working relationship with members of the temporary system.

Delegating responsibility and authority.—Once selected, the

[13]Of course, someone with all those qualities could probably walk on water, too! Still, those *are* important characteristics to look for, and the principal may be able to find a number of persons, each of whom has some of them, so that the temporary system as a whole has these abilities and resources.

191

temporary system's members must be given the authority and responsibility they need to carry out the project. Delegation is perhaps the least understood leadership role. Recall our definition from Chapter 3:

> The principal assigns decision-making responsibility and authority to the staff, perhaps reserving a power of veto or modification. Usually the principal gives a charge that describes specifically the limits of authority, solution requirements, and the range of acceptable solutions.

Delegation is *not* abdication; it *does* mean giving the temporary system clear tasks, goals and limits. Delegation involves giving a charge and specifying non-negotiables.[14]

Giving charges.—Delegation to the temporary system's members should be accompanied by a clear statement of expectations. That allows them to work effectively because they know what their task is; it also makes it more likely that their products will be acceptable to the principal, and it improves relationships because the principal does not need to undo work they've done or reverse decisions they've made.

The task is to state clearly what the temporary system should accomplish; the charge may include any or all of the following points:

1. a deadline for accomplishing the task;
2. the principal's preferred solution—if any—and how strong the principal's preferences are;
3. the principal's power to veto or modify the group's work;
4. non-negotiables and other constraints;
5. what will be done with the group's product after they finish it;
6. requirements about the form of the product;
7. importance of quality vs. acceptance considerations;
8. goals, objectives, and solution requirements;
9. any process considerations, such as who must or may

[14]This information is taken from materials developed for a workshop on decision-management by Consulting Exchange, a private consulting firm.

be involved, what kind of decision-making style is appropriate.

The principal and members of the temporary system need to discuss the charge so that it is understood and accepted by all; members will probably have modifications to suggest.

The "non-negotiables" in point 4 above are policies, rules, political considerations, system norms, and other constraints that limit the temporary system's freedom of action. The task is to state them clearly in advance (as much as possible) so that members of the temporary system know what the "rules of the game" are and can act accordingly.

The principal needs to list as many non-negotiables as he or she can think of and then communicate them to members of the temporary system. They can be encouraged to think of others. Since it is impossible to anticipate all non-negotiables beforehand, build in some checkpoints at which others might be uncovered.

A note: Specifying non-negotiables should be done, but with care. It is only realistic to consider contraints, but principal and staff need to challenge their own beliefs. Often there is a tendency to anticipate trouble in relation to the system and thereby to limit's one's freedom of action more than is actually required. We encourage the principal to take the stance of "I'll try to do it until someone stops me," rather than "I can't do it because they won't let me."

INTEGRATING TEMPORARY SYSTEM AND SCHOOL

Helping members of the temporary system become accepted members of the school involves several actions. One is to give them information about the school and its people. Paper sources of information include faculty and student handbooks, schedules, forms to use, statements of the school's philosophy and goals, etc. More important is information about school climate and norms, such as: dress, use of titles, agreements about openness and discussion of feelings, evaluation systems, how information gets around, and the like. Perhaps the key information is who's who on the staff: teaching assignments, extracurricular responsibilities, committees, and information about opinion leaders, important coalitions, and so on.

Another action is gaining credibility for the project and its staff. That can come by including a project director on the school's management team, personal statements of support by the principal, visibility of the project's activities and aims, and other signals that the project and its staff are important parts of the school.

The final action is designing the various linkages between the project and staff. That means opening up communication channels so that members of the temporary system can give and get information, providing inservice training so that the faculty can use project activities, creating systems for referring students to the project, and devoting time at faculty meetings to discussions of the project.

In this "high task/high relationship" stage, the principal maintains the role of *leader* in structuring tasks and building relationships. The end of the stage comes when the temporary system is set in place; attention shifts from issues of "start-up" to issues of implementing the project's activities.

Stage Three: Development and Implementation

The major tasks of this stage are the creation of materials, trying out new practices in classrooms, and inservice training for teachers and others expected to behave in new ways. It is the stage at which the principal and staff are called on to deliver on the promises made in the proposal. As such it is usually the stage in which unanticipated problems crop up, things don't work out as envisioned, and the impact of the project may call forth adverse reaction from staff, central office, and school board, or community.

THE PRINCIPAL'S ROLE IN IMPLEMENTATION

This stage can be the most frustrating one for the principal, especially if he or she has previously been intensely involved. There can be significant stress arising from a change in level of responsibility, particularly when that means "letting go" and turning over "my thing" to others. The stress is compounded if the principal has doubts about the staff's ability or motivation to implement the project.

Successful principals in our study *did* pull away from day-to-day involvement but continued to support the project staff with expressions of commitment and concrete actions. The extent of the principal's participation depended in part on the size of the school and system. In larger ones, people and resources were available to perform tasks that principals in smaller systems had to do themselves.

Development and implementation is likely to be a "low task/high relationship" stage for the principal, and it is at this stage that the principal most clearly steps out of the role of "leader" and into the role of "manager." Most of the principal's actions will be "backstage" and will be directed mainly to supportive tasks. That may mean that others get most of the credit for the project's accomplishment. As Lao-Tzu (in Townsend, 1970: 81)[15] says, "When the leader's best work is done, the people say, 'We did it ourselves.' "

Having said all that, it is time to remind ourselves and the reader that the low-key, supportive leadership style we have just described is not always appropriate. (Recall the several cases in which the principal described himself as a "facilitator" while the staff complained of a lack of direction and support.) That style is appropriate only if staff members have high enough levels of ability, understanding, and commitment to carry the burden of the project themselves. In cases in which those levels are not sufficiently high, the principal must supply more of the energy, take more of the initiative, and provide more task leadership.

---

[15]We think Townsend's book, *Up the Organization*, has a wealth of ideas for principals and other managers who are more interested in getting the job done than in basking in the title. We would like to see more principals adopt his irreverent style toward bureaucracies and try some of his unorthodox suggestions for treating people humanely and making the organization do its job. He says his book is a "survival manual for successful corporate guerillas."

As the project is implemented, it will begin to have an impact on students, staff, community, and system. The principal will want information about that impact, especially the perceptions and reactions of those most directly affected. About the project, the principal will want to know how it is going, whether it is close to the timetable described in the proposal, and if it is living up to promises and still worth the extra time and effort it takes. Further, the principal will want to know about unanticipated problems that have arisen and whether adjustments in the project's goals, activities, timeline, or budget will have to be made.

As to staff, the principal will want to know how project activities are received by the staff and their students. Are there rifts between project and non-project staff?

Finally, the principal will want information about the reactions of key decision-makers in the system and in the community. What are their perceptions of the project and their responses to it? Do they have valid information about the project?

INTERACTING WITH STAFF

The most important interactions with staff are arranging for inservice and providing a variety of kinds of support.

Inservice training.—Implementing the project will usually require some kind of inservice training. The Rand studies found that the more training, the better. The most effective training was found to be very concrete "how-to-do-it" workshops given by local people; outside technical assistants were

---

[16]The Rand finding echoes other conclusions which indicate that teachers prefer to receive inservice training from someone who is "like us." Teachers are usually more successful at training teachers than are administrators or supervisors, who in turn are generally more successful than outside consultants or university professors. The dilemma, of course, is what to do when qualified teachers are not available to train staff. In our experience, the strategy most likely to succeed is an "inside/outside" combination team. That team comprises both practicing teachers who have technical skills in implementing the project, knowledge of the system (or a similar one), and credibility, combined with inservice providers or consultants who have skills in designing and delivering inservice education and problem-solving for adults.

generally not effective in the training role, according to Greenwood, Mann, and McLaughlin (1975).[16] Some training may be required to give people technical skills, while other training may need to be directed at improving relationship skills, group processes, and working procedures.

Sometimes the principal will give the inservice training himself or herself, but more often the principal will arrange for the inservice to be conducted by others. Teachers we interviewed told us of a variety of helpful actions that principals took. They included arranging for visits to other schools, arranging the school's schedule to make participation in inservice convenient for teachers, shortening the school day to give time to plan for the project, and training community volunteers so that they would fit smoothly into the school.

Providing support and feedback.—We have noted that teachers mentioned "giving social support and active participation" most often as a helpful behavior of the principal, and we discussed a variety of ways to give support.

One thing the principal needs to know is what kinds of support project staff and others need to remain clear in their understanding of the project and to maintain the expenditure of energy for it. That could mean encouraging words, social-emotional support, recognition, reinforcement; it could also mean objective information on which to base judgments about the effect of the project and the value of thier efforts; it could mean, too, anticipating and organizing odd jobs that need doing—making copies of materials, arranging transportation schedules, securing permits, or serving coffee—so that staff can concentrate on the core tasks of the project. The kinds of things people find supportive and reinforcing differ from person to person, so the principal's sensitivity to what those things are—perhaps satisfying achievement, affiliation, or influence needs—is important.

An important consideration is whether people who are not involved in the project feel that they are receiving an equitable share of the principal's support and attention, as well as more tangible resources. One often hears that people in the project

197

get "special favors," such as lower class loads or extra materials that are not available to non-project staff. The principal should be able to document the resources that both project and non-project staff get, make sure that there is an equitable distribution, or have a very good reason why the project gets disproportionate resources.

People we interviewed told us of many supportive actions by principals. Some were general statements such as: the principal demonstrated confidence in the faculty; he built trust with the faculty; she created and maintained staff ownership in the project. Other actions expressed support for staff and the project director, by recognizing outstanding contributions of teachers, by hosting social gatherings to give the project visibility, by expressing thanks to the project staff, and by otherwise demonstrating encouragement and recognition. Still others involved feedback, by helping people assess their own teaching styles, by making the effort to find out from teachers how they were doing, and by giving teachers feedback on how the principal felt teachers were doing. Finally, staff appreciated demonstrations of the principal's commitment that included his or her participation in inservice training for the project, sitting in on project meetings, being a sounding board or advisor and helper when problems came up, and performing a variety of "chief cook and bottle washer" kinds of tasks.

In all, people in the projects we studied wanted to have some ownership and responsibility for the project, which required the principal to step back into a less active role, but they also wanted to see and hear signs that the principal still considered the project important and valued their efforts.

Finally, the principal has to be aware of both the symbolism and substance of resources. Resources take on symbolic value when they are viewed as signals about who and what is important in the school. The principal needs to be clear, perhaps by stating the intention overtly, when allocating resources so that the signal that is perceived is the one the principal intends to send.

We have said that three key roles of the principal are being an *advocate* for the project, a *linker* between the project and the system, and a *resource* acquirer. Those are the roles played by principals in dealing with the system and environment during this stage.

Advocacy.—As the project begins to have an impact on students, then parents, central office administrators, and others will have favorable or unfavorable reactions to it. The principal will be called on to be an advocate for the project before audiences such as parent groups, the superintendent, the school board, and—if there is a continuation proposal—the funding agency. Doing so effectively requires the abilities to gather information, speak knowledgeably, and use interpersonal skills such as negotiation that we described earlier.

Linkage.—In many ways, the principal's most important interactions are those with groups other than the faculty and project staff. The principal is generally the school's link to the central office and to other parts of the environment, such as the funding agency. Being an effective linker requires having information about the project and its needs, knowing the location of information and other resources in the system and environment, and being able to hook the project up with them. That may involve, for example, the principal's working with departments such as the business or personnel office to smooth things for the project.

Acquiring resources.—We have little to add here to our previous discussions about acquiring resources, except to note that at times the resources needed will be materials or other physical objects, at other times intangible resources such as information, approval, or legitimacy, and at still other times "person-power," such as the aides actively recruited by Martin Lawrence in Case 3 or the community volunteers trained by Warren Redford in Case 7.

Stage Four: Ending and Institutionalization

The stage of ending and institutionalization is a figure with two faces, one looking backward and the other looking forward. It is an ending and there are numerous tasks to be done such as evaluation, final reports, making sure the budget is in order, and so on. But it is also a new stage in the life of the project, one in which it makes the transition from an experiment ("we're trying to see how it works") to a routine ("the way we do things here"). Institutionalization therefore cycles through many of the decisions and issues of earlier stages. There are decisions to be made about what parts of the project will remain, about securing resources to continue it, and about making new accommodations to incorporate the project into the on-going life of the school.

THE PRINCIPAL'S ROLE

The level of activity of the principal generally increases as the project draws to a close. While "development and implementation" was generally a "low task/high relationship" stage, task considerations become important again as the project ends.

The principal will want trustworthy information about what parts of the project have proven beneficial and what parts have not. Some of that information will come from formal evaluation instruments used in the project, while some of it will come from discussions of the project in faculty meetings or informal discussions with project staff and faculty. Thus, the principal needs to know what information about the project's outcomes is available, where that information is located, and whether methods used to get it are dependable.

That information is important to the decision about what to continue, to "institutionalize." How that decision is made depends largely on the school's customary style of making decisions about curriculum and other matters. In some schools it is a "telling" decision which the principal announces to the faculty; in other schools faculty are more involved in those kinds of decisions. Our preference is to involve faculty in those decisions. Faculty in one project we studied but did not describe in Chapter 2 said that the principal helped by making a firm decision about what was to remain and then by convincing department chairpersons to approve her assignment of faculty from their regular allotments to support it.

INTERACTION WITH FACULTY

The principal will want to reassess the faculty's readiness, this time in terms of their ability and commitment to carrying out the worthwhile parts of the project after outside funding stops. That may mean doing some problem-solving to make accommodations for the project in the on-going routine of the school. It may also mean that inservice training in the project might be needed if teachers who were previously not involved will now be asked to incorporate the project activities into their classrooms. And it may also mean a new search for resources.

Both beginnings and endings are stressful, and this stage entails a little of the stress of both. Project staff may feel stressed because their jobs are ending or their roles are being redefined. Teachers may feel stressed when project resources they relied on are withdrawn, or because they will be asked to behave in new ways. The principal can be a source of interpersonal and material support by being empathic and by taking action to help others acquire resources, explore alternatives, and make decisions.

DEALING WITH THE SYSTEM

Nearly all the issues of acquiring approval and other kinds of resources from the system and the environment recur at this stage. That is especially true when resources from the district are required to maintain the project after outside funding ends.

Actually, the principal should begin before this stage to develop support for the project. Decision-makers must often think as much as a year ahead in preparing budgets, for example. Funding agencies who might pick up the project often have similarly long lead times. And it is essential to cultivate a network of relationships and sources of support in the system and environment so that they can be counted on when the time comes.

This chapter has been addressed to principals. We discussed leadership styles within the framework of Hersey and Blachard's "Situational Leadership Theory," we described the skills we think are necessary to successful project management, and we identified the actions that we think should be taken to move the project through the four stages of its life cycle. In the final chapter we direct our discussion to staff development specialists and others who provide inservice training for administrators. In it we present our recommendations for making that training effective and relevant to the needs of principals who manage externally funded projects.

CHAPTER 5

Recommendations for Inservice Training

Everybody talks about inservice education, some people are doing something about it, but virtually no one agrees with anyone else about what it is and should be. For instance, administrators and people responsible for inservice training met in May 1979 at a workshop on school administrator training sponsored by the Office of the Assistant Secretary for Education. *Education USA* (May 21, 1979: 289) reported that there was no agreement among participants about either the content or format of administrator training. The only two points of agreement were that administrator training should be directed to principals and that it must have the full support of the superintendent and school board. One participant noted: "Since training for principals continues, for the most part, to focus on the tasks and functions necessary to maintaining schools, principals are now in need of training that will equip them with the intellectual and human relations skills necessary to manage improvement efforts in their schools." But most training does not meet that need of principals; as one elementary principal from Virginia complained: "It is very discouraging for administrators to participate in sessions where the basic assumption is that they are just then learning how to spell 'education' . . . don't assume that everyone needs the same dose of medicine."

We don't think most principals need to learn how to spell "education." One of the purposes of this study was to find out from principals and others just what principals think they need. We asked what inservice activities were associated with the 14 projects we studied and how they worked. If none was offered, we asked what kind of training people though *would* have been helpful. We also asked people about their past experience with training and staff development and what they thought about those experiences. Finally, we asked people to describe their ideas about what kinds of training or experience would be most helpful to principals in managing externally funded projects. In this chapter we describe what we learned; we also present our recommendations for the content and delivery of inservice education for principals.

The Scope of the Problem

There are not many ways in which principals can acquire the skills we listed in Chapter 4. There is little in the way of experience as a teacher, administrative certification programs, or current inservice offerings that prepares the principal to manage projects.

Sarason (1971: 112) notes that the principal's experience as a teacher rarely prepares her or him for the administrator's position: "The fact that a teacher has spent a number of years in a classroom *with children* is no compelling basis for assuming that it prepares one for a position in which one's major task is working *with adults*. Put another way: being a 'leader' of children, and exclusively of children, does not necessarily prepare one for being a leader of adults." Teachers, over a period of years, come to absorb and accept a tradition of the way things "should be" in schools, and it is unlikely that they will be disposed to change that tradition when they become principals: "In fact, one of the major criteria for choosing a principal is that they were 'good' teachers and good refers not only to the quality of their teaching but also to their implicit acceptance of the way things are" (Sarason, 1971: 113). He suggests, in conclusion, that neither the teacher's experience, nor the person's motivations for becoming a principal, nor the criteria normally used to select principals give reason to believe that the principalship will be used as a vehicle for educational change and innovation.

Another potential source of training for administrators is the preservice certification programs they must take. Becker et al. (1971: 7)[1] conclude that most of those programs do little to prepare principals for educational leadership:

> In colleges and universities the prepatory programs for the . . . principalship appear to be relics of a past age. Course content seems to emphasize studies "about" education. There is little evidence that any real consideration has been given to the experiences that will develop in prospective . . . principals the knowledge, skills, and critical insights (that they need).

They found that most preparatory programs seemed to be geared toward obsolete management practices. While principals surveyed consistently indentified human relationships as their most crucial problem, there was little emphasis in certification programs on learning those skills or learning about effective change. As a result, the "majority of principals are confident of their ability to oversee the routine operation of their buildings, but relatively few have any degree of confidence in their ability to assume a leadership role in instructional improvement" (Becker et al., 1971: 9).

Another source of learning for principals might be inservice training and other experiences provided by universities, administrators' associations, regional laboratories, and other state or regional agencies. Becker et al. comment that principals are rarely aware of those resources; they also question the adequacy of the services themselves. From the results of their national survey, they conclude that principals' associations were simply not organized to provide effective and specific help; state departments of education were more interested in their regulatory functions or in disseminating information that served their own purposes; universities offered little beyond traditional campus courses; regional laboratories were not usually accessible to the majority of principals; and federal

[1]The name of their study has to be one of the *great* titles in the educational literature: *Elementary Principals and Their Schools: Beacons of Brilliance and Potholes of Pestilence.*

education departments were so far removed from the local school as to be useless to principals.

At its most extreme, the impoverishment of inservice experiences available to principals is reflected in two statements. The first is a principal's description of meetings of the state administrators' association: "We sit around and tell lies and brag about the things we would like to do but are not doing and then in the evenings we play poker" (Becker et al. 1971: 85). The second is by a university official commenting on his institution's investment in administrators' inservice: "The only inservice we provide for our graduates is to pray for them" (Becker et al. 1971: 121).

Given that situation, it should be of little wonder that so many principals are so ill prepared to assume leadership of externally funded projects. We found that principals had trouble even *thinking* about what kind of inservice would be useful to them.

Principals and others had considerable difficulty in answering our questions about the topic of inservice and staff development for administrators. Many persons did not seem to be answering the questions we asked; a common response was to give us ideas for teacher inservice or to make suggestions about how principals could provide inservice for teachers. We believe their difficulty mirrors the lack of thought and emphasis that has been given to what principals need.

We were also somewhat disturbed to hear that, when principals considered what kind of inservice would be useful for them, they rarely gave careful, reflective thought about the behaviors needed to manage externally funded projects, the kinds of skills they needed, and ways to deliver training to them. Instead, the topics of inservice education most frequently mentioned were those that seemed to be currently "hot" topics or fads—time and stress management, and so on. For example, one principal thought that the most valuable inservice experience he had had was a course in cardiopulmonary resuscitation. He thought that it was more important than "even a course in reading methods, because having a CPR person in the building might save a life."

Our intent is not to criticize the principals and others we interviewed. We are not distressed by their lack of imagination about inservice so much as we are disturbed that staff development specialists and other persons who provide inservice education (that is, people like us) have failed to convey to principals a useful conception of how inservice education can have something helpful to say about the critical demands and stresses of their jobs. Inservice education for administrators lags far behind what is available to teachers. There are Teacher Corps and Teacher Centers, but where are the Principal Corps and the Principal Centers?[2] Some guidance to identifying the inservice needs of principals—but not much—comes from recent surveys.

Surveying Staff Development Needs of Principals

Several agencies have surveyed principals about their inservice needs during the past few years. In one school district in Oregon, 82 principals were asked to identify the types of workshops they would find most helpful in developing their skills (Callan, 1979). The items most frequently mentioned were: skills in decision-making; conflict-resolution techniques; life planning for administrators; and procedures for improving school-community relations. The Confederation of Oregon School Administrators (1978) surveyed information from 431 principals and found that the five most commonly identified needs were: evaluating instructional programs; staff development and renewal; improving school climate; curriculum renewal and development; and staff evaluation. Similarly, 51 principals of schools with Teacher Corps projects in California

[2]Perhaps the best recent review of the state of the art in teacher inservice education is the series of reports published by the Inservice Teacher Education Concepts Project. A recent guide to the literature of inservice education for teachers is *Sources and Resources: An Annotated Bibliography on Inservice Education* (Revised Ed.) prepared by Kathleen Porter and the staff of the National Council of States on Inservice Education. It can be procured from the National Dissemination Center, Syracuse University, 123 Huntington Hall, Syracuse, New York 13210.

were surveyed in 1978 and 1979. The highest priority needs in 1978 were: evaluating instructional personnel; dealing with discipline; improving student learning; improving school-community relations; and team-building at the school level. The 1979 list included: curriculum improvement; evaluating educational programs; catalysts for promoting change; problem-solving and decision-making; working with parents, faculty, and students; and instructional leadership and staff development. A national survey of principals managing Teacher Corps projects (Latta, 1978) showed that principals' training needs clustered around three themes: how to deal with the community, organizational skills, and how to deal with diminishing resources while trying to promote change.

In our view, the results of those surveys resemble the concerns that we found among principals and others in the projects we studied. Among the common themes are: exercising leadership in educational improvement and change; evaluating instructional programs and personnel; maintaining good school-community relations; providing staff development and improving school climate; and developing specific procedures such as problem-solving, decision-making, and conflict resolution. Those topics of concern could serve as alternative titles for many of the issues and problems we identified: gathering information; advocating the project to the community; assessing and enhancing the staff's readiness to undertake special projects; and so on.

We found that the comments of principals and others we interviewed about inservice education provided us with information about four topics: opportunities for staff development of principals that were offered in the projects; prior staff development and training experiences; problems principals had experienced with inservice; and recommendations for the content and delivery of inservice training for principals. We next report those findings.

PROJECT OPPORTUNITIES FOR INSERVICE

All but two of the fourteen cases we studied offered some

208

kind of inservice. In six cases inservice was available to both principals and teachers, but it usually dealt with the content of the project. Only in two cases was inservice developed specifically for administrators, but in neither case were principals given inservice in the kinds of leadership and management responsibilities that we have discussed.

PRIOR STAFF DEVELOPMENT AND TRAINING EXPERIENCES

Some of the principals we interviewed had attended "hundreds" of inservice events during their many years of experience, while others had been to virtually none. As a group, they mentioned relatively few different kinds of inservice that they had attended.

Three persons mentioned workshops and conferences sponsored by the state administrators' association on topics such as management techniques, stress, programs for gifted students, accreditation, and middle schools. Four persons mentioned programs sponsored by the local district; topics included stress, time management, conflict resolution, contract negotiation, and communication skills.

Other activities (these were mentioned only once each) were sponsored by a university, a regional educational laboratory, a private business, and a national professional organization. They were seminars, workshops, or conferences on leadership training, group processes, academic courses, and CPR techniques.

PROBLEMS OF INSERVICE

Not surprisingly, the administrators we interviewed were critical of the inservice they had received. Some complained that the inservice had been "too theoretical" or irrelevant to their daily work, had out-of-date or "incredibly dry" instructors, and had been held at inconvenient times which interfered either with their work at school or their leisure time.

Their criticism of inservice included poor timing (mentioned 7 times), content that was not relevant to the leadership

209

of schools (6), lack of incentives (4), the location, duration, or organization of the event (3), poor quality of instructors and presentations (3), inappropriate participants (3), lack of district support and encouragement (2), and just being "burned out on workshops." Two persons said they did not personally value inservice.

Nor was there any consensus on how the inservice should be delivered. For example, there was no agreement on what times were most appropriate and convenient for principals, or for the kind of format that would be most helpful.

RECOMMENDATIONS FOR INSERVICE

Principals and others had a variety of recommendatons about the content and delivery of inservice, as well as its participants and sponsors. Those needs generally fell into five categories: those specific to the project itself, organizational improvement skills, general management skills, specific administrative tasks, and some miscellaneous items. There was little concensus on the items: only "interpersonal communication skills" (11 times), "knowledge of project goals" (6), and "knowledge of change strategies" (7), were mentioned more than five times. We have therefore not noted how many times each item was mentioned; our aim is primarily to show the variety and range of responses.

Figure 6 presents a summary of the responses of principals and of other persons interviewed. As we review this list, we note that principals and others identified some of the same needs for skills that we described in Chapter 4, but not all of them. We and they were in agreement on needs for technical knowledge and skills related directly to the project, problem-solving abilities of various kinds, interpersonal communications skills, leadership, and clarifying expectations. Persons interviewed did not directly identify the needs we saw for skills in self-awareness, conceptual abilities, resource or information acquisition, or giving feedback. That may mean that we and they were simply using different words to describe the same thing. It may also mean that we and they have

different ways of translating "helpful and unhelpful behaviors" into needs for inservice. It probably also means that
we and they look at the world in different ways; we shall have
more to say about that difference later in this chapter.

FIGURE 6

Recommendations for Satisfying Inservice Needs of Principals

Categories of Needs	By Principals	By Others
Inservice specific to project	Role expectations and time needed Practical knowledge of subject area	Desired goals and outcomes Mandates and guidelines General knowledge of project Budget Project materials
Organizational improvement	Interpersonal communication Knowledge of change strategies Using resources Group processes Delegation and shared management	Motivational skills and involving staff Understanding power and influence Problem-solving and decision-making Conducting meetings
General management	Evaluation systems Management Program implementation Organizing curriculum Budgeting	Organizational planning and long-range planning
Specific administrative tasks	Time and priorities management Proposal writing Supervision Discipline	Needs assessment Dissemination Conflict management
Miscellaneous	Needs of the specific administrator How to present inservice to teachers "Nitty gritty" subjects Working with teachers	Understanding management modes Glasser-type training

We also asked people to comment on the kinds of delivery
that they thought could reach audiences of principals. Their
suggestions fell into four categories: format, structure, location, and sponsorship. The most frequently made suggestion
was that of visiting other schools. With that exception, there

211

was little agreement, and no other item was mentioned more than five times. Here are their suggestions. (Within each category the suggestions are listed in order of number of times mentioned.)

Format: credit courses on a regular basis, workshops, week-long training sessions that include people from across the state, national meetings, retreats, opportunities to exchange with business or other schools, interviews, discussions, peer consultations, conferences, two-way evaluation and feedback with teachers, and video-programmed courses.

Structure: small group sessions (rather than individual training), mandated inservice written into proposals with options of choice for the principal, regularly scheduled inservice days for principals, and "hands on" experiences.

Location: visits to other schools, places away from the school, events held at the school.

Sponsors and participants: participation by both teachers and administrators, presentations by skilled people, experiences provided by an intermediate education agency or district or college, supervision by the superintendent that includes help in setting goals, sponsorship by the state education department, including teachers and community members in administrators' inservice, and activities with other administrators.

We have a variety of reactions to the statements of people we interviewed about their history with inservice, problems they had experienced, and recommendations. The first is that most people seemed to conceive of inservice in traditional ways, viewing it mainly as "something that somebody does to you in a workshop." They did not make as strong a connection as we did between the behaviors of principals and inservice training needs, especially as that training might be delivered in ways other than workshops and conferences. Second, while some suggestions focused on the need to give principals knowledge of the specific content or concerns of the project itself, there was little explicit mention of a need to increase principals' skills in performing the behaviors that were found

212

helpful to projects. (We think, though, that awareness of that need is implicit in many of the suggestions for inservice; we obviously think it is present in people's discussion of the behaviors themselves.) Third, we think that there is a certain lack of awareness of the full range of inservice possibilities, to judge from the responses; people generally thought of inservice in terms of traditionally taught topics or ones which are current fads. People seemed to be thinking in terms of what inservice usually is, or what is currently popular, rather than conceptualizing inservice as a specific response to identified needs. Finally, the sheer variety of responses is itself instructive. It confirms our impression that the fourteen principals varied widely in their understanding of special projects and change processes, leadership, and their abilities to implement change. It also reinforces our belief that there is no one best content, delivery method, or type of inservice that will match the needs of a diverse group of administrators such as the one we studied. It is to a presentation of our recommendations, based on that belief, that we now turn.

Recommendations to Inservice Providers

In this section we present a number of recommendations for providing inservice education that will enhance principals' abilities to manage externally funded projects. Many of our recommendations are based directly on what principals said they wanted. Others are based on our inferences about what kind of training we think would be useful, according to our interpretations of the case studies; our reading of the literature on educational change, the role of the principal, change processes, and inservice education; and our own experiences in providing inservice to teachers and administrators and in conducting our own externally funded projects.

CONTEXT OF THE RECOMMENDATIONS

The conceptual framework that guides our thinking about inservice education is a "Responsive Inservice Education" model which has grown out of our experiences with our own two Teacher Corps projects and our experiences as teachers, administrators, project participants, and inservice providers.

Ours is not a "put tab A in slot B" kind of model that prescribes certain actions; rather, it is a set of values, beliefs, and ways of thinking about consultation, training, and technical assistance. Lovell (1980: 14–15) describes the key ideas of responsive inservice:

> Responsive inservice education is a way of thinking, conceiving, and planning that provides a rationale for a specific method of acting in regard to inservice education.
>
> The key word is "responsive"—the heart of the concept of responsive inservice is the determining of the needs of the learners and addressing those needs directly, specifically, and concretely.
>
> Responsive inservice education is planned for specific people in a specific site and takes into account the factors in that setting that differentiate it from others. The clients and providers of the inservice experience are actively involved in all phases of development of the inservice activity.
>
> The design and delivery evolve from careful identification of the client(s), the problem or need to be addressed, the constraints (time, materials, setting, etc.), the resources, the assumptions, and the desired outcomes. The client(s) and the provider negotiate key aspects of the experience: participation, objectives, content, delivery, desired outcomes, evaluation, and follow-up.

We think that our approach offers distinct advantages, while it also incurs some costs. Among the advantages, it is congruent with the characteristics of adult learners because it recognizes their experience and expertise. It increases the probability that the training will actually attend to identified needs because clients influence the process. It is flexible, because the inservice provider can use a variety of methods. It is likely to develop participants' commitment to the learning experience because they develop ownership in the process and product. We think it is efficient in the sense of "the most direct route to the achievement of specified goals," although it is not time efficient in the sense of "the quickest way to do something that's somehow related to general goals."

Responsive inservice education, as we conceive it, is likely to be more expensive than mass instruction in actual dollars,

214

although we think it can be cost efficient because it is more likely that participants will actually use the inservice experience in their daily work. It is somewhat costly in terms of time, since it requires sometimes substantial negotiations between the provider and the receiver of inservice. It also makes the inservice provider open herself or himself up to influence from participants, which can be an uncomfortable experience for someone unaccustomed to sharing control over inservice activities. It may not be an appropriate strategy when inservice activities stem from mandates and decisions about which there is no room for change or negotiation so that "responsiveness" and "flexibility" would be sheer pretense. Finally, it may not be applicable when the administrative support and resources for it are not available.

In short, just as we believe that there is no one best leadership style or role for principals, we similarly believe that there is no one best content, format, or style for administrative inservice. It depends on a careful analysis of who the client is, what the tasks are, and what is the setting within which the inservice will occur. Our first recommendation, then, is that inservice for principals be based on the strategy we have found effective:

> *Recommendation #1:* Keep any staff development responsive to local conditions and individualized to specific principals' abilities.

It is tempting to recommend the development of training materials and workshops that could be conducted on a national level and that principals with externally funded projects could be encouraged or required to attend. We think that strategy would be a mistake.

The principals we studied in just fourteen cases had a broad range of experience and ability. Some were newcomers to externally funded projects, while others had a long and successful history of managing them. Some thoroughly understood change processes in schools, while others did not. Those differences, we believe, have to be taken into account in the design and delivery of inservice. In short, we agree with the principal we quoted at the beginning of this chapter: "don't assume that everyone needs the same dose of medicine."

CHALLENGING ASSUMPTIONS

Any human action—and that includes providing inservice for principals—is based in part on images and assumptions about things such as human nature, values about what is good, and beliefs about what works. We think that a depressingly large proportion of preservice and inservice training is based on faulty assumptions, so that millions of inservice dollars are spent to no good effect. We challenge inservice providers, including ourselves, to examine and test their assumptions.

For all practical purposes, most inservice providers and most school principals live in two different cultures, and those different cultures can produce very different ways of looking at the world. As Sarason (1971: 15) notes: "the observer is not neutral. By virtue of the fact that the observer is himself part of a structure — be it in the school culture or in one outside of it — his perception and thinking are in various ways incomplete, selective, and distorted." It is all too easy for the inservice provider to focus too narrowly on his or her own area of concern or expertise and to lose sight of the many and complex forces with which principals and teachers struggle daily. Becoming the captive of one's own perspective and assumptions, rather than being sensitive to what principals and others are saying, can lead the inservice provider to believe that she or he has "the answer" which would solve the problem if principals would just listen. Too much reliance on one's own untested assumptions can lead the inservice provider to approach principals with the attitude, "I know what's wrong with you and I know how to fix you up." It is then very dismaying when one's brilliant ideas are not enthusiastically accepted by the people one is trying desperately to help.

To be more specific, most staff development specialists and other inservice providers are what Harry Wolcott (1977) calls "technocrats" instead of "teachers." Those two groups seem almost to live in two different cultures.[3] Each has its own

216

language, assumptions, values, and ways of dealing with the world; the differences between the two can often lead to misunderstanding or conflict.

The distinguishing characteristics of the technocratic culture are its emphases on rationality and purposefulness. A recurring theme in technocrats' talk is that of arranging the world in neat and orderly (i.e., rational) ways. That is possible in large part because technocrats have the luxury of being able to create simplified models of the world—ones which isolate particular aspects of reality—and then acting on the world in light of those models. (It is also handy that technocrats usually get to make up the rules by which the models are constructed.) The second distinguishing characteristic is purposefulness: the technocrat will nearly always begin by struggling to come to precise definitions of the problem and goals, and then by constructing a set of activities to reach those goals. One result, Wolcott notes, is that technocrats often deal with solvable problems instead of important ones. Another hallmark of the culture of technocrats is a belief in progress; to a technocrat, "there is no question that whatever is being done now can be done better. The only questions is where to begin" (Wolcott, 1977: 160). Finally, technocrats believe in having information that one can use to define problems and set goals.[4]

Principals and teachers, in contrast, live in much more close and intimate contact with the "blooming, buzzing confusion" of the complex reality of everyday life in the school. They tend to conceptualize their world and their goals in rather global and imprecise ways. They are bound by dealing with the pressing realities of the present. They respond more to the shifting patterns of concrete actions, momentary disruptions of the always fragile routine, and the concerns of interpersonal relationships than to the neatly ordered generalizations of

[3]To be precise, Wolcott, in *Teachers versus Technocrats*, refers to the two groups as "moieties," a technical term that anthropologists use to describe two distinct halves of the same culture.

[4]The reader, of course, will recognize that the authors of this book are dedicated technocrats in Wolcott's usage of the term.

technocrats. They deal with short-term problems that seem to require immediate solutions, and often deal with those problems by creating ad hoc solutions, a never-ending arrangement of coalitions and negotiated agreements, and temporary answers that must be reconstructed when the same concern surfaces later in a slightly different form. Wolcott points out that while technocrats deal with teachers through stable administrative structures, hierarchies of tasks, and knowledge, "teachers seem to cope with technocrats through temporary *ad hoc* arrangements about as sophisticated as a Plains Indian raiding party" (Wolcott, 1977: 167). One result is that it is rare that principals or teachers step back from the immediate situation to examine and challenge their own assumptions, goals, and customary ways of doing things. Goodlad (in Sarason, 1971: 118–19) concluded after many talks with people in schools: "Neither principals nor teachers were able to articulate clearly just what they thought to be the most important for their schools to accomplish. And neither group was very clear on changes that should be effected in the future."

Our intention is not to disparage the one culture or the other; nor is it to advocate that teachers become technocrats or vice versa. Each culture has its own strengths (but every strength is its own weakness). We generally share the technocrats' belief that many things now being done in schools can be done better, and that solutions will require large measures of rational planning based on valid information. At the same time, we and a few other technocrats are beginning to realize that our "rational" view of schools and changing them is in many ways less than worthless; in many cases it has gotten in the way of intelligent action. Clark (1980: 13) says "goal-based, rational planning systems fail not because they are implemented inadequately but because they are inappropriate conceptualizations of the organizations they are intended to portray. They are rigorous, solid structures built on a foundation of sand." Organizational theorists and others are coming to describe schools as "loosely coupled systems" or as "organized anarchies," and to use terms like "garbage-can model of decision-making." In short, theorists are in ways coming to accept the "messy" conceptualization of schools that principals and teachers have held all along.

At the same time, the "teacher culture" is strong in being sensitive to the complexities and tenuousness of life in schools, and principals are usually more aware of the political and interpersonal restraints on their action than the inservice providers who try to help them. Yet persons in the teacher-culture of the school are also often so caught up in the day-to-day routine that they start doing things for the sake of doing things, without questioning the purposes and assumptions guiding their actions. They are often easily distracted by the latest gimmicks and fads in inservice education without stopping to think about what their needs are. Those observations on the two cultures lead us to our second recommendation:

> *Recommendation #2:* Recognize that inservice providers and principals often have very different perspectives. Bridge the gap by challenging your own assumptions about schools and by negotiating goals and activities of inservice with clients.

Wellman (1980: 8) points out that much inservice training for managers is based on assumptions such as: "organizations have well-defined goals"; "organizations can be run rationally"; "effective leadership can be measured." Noting—like Clark—that these assumptions rarely reflect what the school is really like, she offers three "counter-assumptions":

1. Organizations do not have well-defined goals. Managers are more often faced with making decisions when goals are unclear than when they are clear.
2. Organizational rationality and predictability are myths. Managers are in charge of organized anarchies.
3. Effective leadership is largely dependent on interpersonal skills. We are not able to accurately define or measure the effect of most interpersonal skills. Intuition, another non-measurable phenomenon, is an important variable in what makes an "effective" manager.

In all, we think that the assumptions guiding most models for

219

planning inservice education are erroneous. That is one reason why we emphasize the importance of negotiating expectations, goals, procedures, and intended outcomes with the groups we work with; it is one way of challenging and refining our own assumptions.

THE PRINCIPAL AS ADULT LEARNER

Some important assumptions in inservice are those that shape the inservice provider's conception of the persons with whom she or he works. Too often, inservice providers apparently operate on the assumption that all learners are alike, that all learners are beginners, or that the needs of experienced professionals are the same as those of preservice or beginning teachers.[5] That inservice education should recognize the different experiences of participants and capitalize on their expertise leads us to our third recommendation:

Recommendation #3: Provide the mature professional with something more than new understandings and skills; integrate work, education, and leisure into training and consultative events.

We have already made clear the importance that we place on the motives of *achievement, affiliation,* and *influence.* (Our thinking has been strongly influenced by the work of Maslow, 1954; Alderfer, 1969; McClelland, 1958; and Schmuck, Runkel, Arends, and Arends, 1977.) We have found that clients[6]

---

[5]A principal of our acquaintance recently returned from a national conference for schools with externally funded projects. She was irate because, as she put it, "First one idiot got up in front of a group of experienced principals and lectured to us about how important parents are to kids. Then another one used a lot of slides and charts to give us the amazing news that our schools had not only formal but also informal structures and networks." She did not leave the conference with a high regard for either the lecturers or the funding agency.

[6]The use of the term "client" is at best an awkward accommodation. While the term does serve to distinguish those who "receive" inservice from those who "provide" it, the word can carry unfortunate connotations. It seems to designate principals and others merely as the passive recipients of the inservice provider's services. That connotation clearly violates the collaborative spirit and strategy of responsive inservice education as we know it. We have not, however, been able to find an acceptable substitute, so we continue to use the term, with reservations.

of inservice will remain motivated and responsive if they experience success rather than failure, if they have influence over important parts of the inservice, and if they experience friendship and collegiality rather than isolation or subordination.

From our reading of several theorists on adult development, we think there are four important characteristics that distinguish mature professionals from their younger, beginning colleagues.

First, mature professionals need more than new understandings and skills for their repertoire. Instead, they will seek to integrate in new ways the knowledge, experiences, and skills they already possess. They will look for inservice programs that allow them to clarify career options, to increase their interpersonal competencies, and to actualize their potential not only as professionals but also as whole persons.

Second, adult learners seek ways to integrate into their inservice experiences with aspects of life that are usually viewed separately—work, education, and leisure. We think that is particularly true for professionals who consider restructured jobs, sabbaticals, job-sharing, and other new forms of work.

Third, mature professionals need collegiality rather than criticism from inservice providers. Feeling that their experience counts for something, they will not endure criticism or activities that spotlight their deficiencies with the submissiveness of the college sophomore. Instead, they will seek inservice providers who respect their experience and who will help them build on it to learn new things.

Finally, mature inservice participants retain the responsibility for integrating theory and practice in their own way, and according to their own needs. It is not an appropriate strategy to design "principal-proof packages" and expect participants to accept them whole without consideration for their particular situations. Rather, inservice providers and participants need to be flexible and responsive to each other during the inservice process, modifying the process of giving and receiving assistance as their personal relationship develops.

221

THE CONTENT OF INSERVICE

We do not have a great deal to say about the specific content of inservice, because we heed our own advice that it must be tailor-made for specific situations. We do, however, have some suggestions.

First, the lists of critical issues and infromation, roles of the principal, and sets of skills that we summarized at the end of Chapter 4 should be one starting point in establishing an agenda for inservice for principals with externally funded projects. Training, consultation, and technical assistance could be planned by principal and provider after consideration of which of those topics are most relevant to the particular situation. One activity might be to use adaptations of those lists as self-assessment forms to help principals clarify their values and preferences. Other activities could help principals develop the interpersonal communication skills that many people we interviewed said were important. Other kinds of training could help principals devise ways of collecting information about school, staff, and system.

Wellman (1980: 9–25) offers several suggestions for administrative inservice that we find compatible with our thinking. Here are the most salient of her ideas:

1. Training in how to question one's assumption and to conceptualize problems.
2. Acquiring information about organizational complexity and "messiness," together with ways to conceptualize and deal with complex systems.
3. Learning how to make decisions in the midst of uncertainty.
4. Dealing with stress by reconceptualization and creative problem-solving to deal with ambiguity and uncertainty.
5. Acquiring skills in interpersonal communication, conflict management, developing trust, and introspection.
6. Learning ways to organize and manage one's time, energy, and attention.

7. Learning how to recognize and use the symbolic importance of seemingly mundane issues (as, for example, resource allocation).
8. Finding out where to go for help, including consumer education about consultants and providers of inservice education

Many of her suggestions—based on a reading of recent literature on organizational complexity—mirror our own. Some principals will feel a need for the kinds of abilities that Wellman discusses; other principals will feel needs associated with other issues. In general, we think that issues addressed by inservice fall into one of these four categories:

1. *Technical.*—Inservice providers are often asked to give assistance in technical issues such as instructional techniques, curriculum development, and related topics. This category includes training in the specific content of a project or procedures required by the funding agency.
2. *Procedural.*—When people come together to accomplish tasks, they must establish procedures or ground rules for how to work together. Examples include making agreements about the role of the principal and others in relation to the project, or clarifying expectations about giving and receiving feedback.
3. *Process.*—Regardless of the skills of individuals and the procedures of groups, problems can be encountered in the "people part" of a project. Relevant training would include interpersoanl communications skills, conflict management, etc.
4. *Morale/Cohesion.*—Staffs often encounter difficulties in maintaining a climate of trust, helpfulness, and caring. Training could be directed at ways to maintain enthusiasm, give social support, and so on.

THE DELIVERY OF INSERVICE EDUCATION

Some of the ways of delivering inservice education will remain as they have for years past, and that is not necessarily a

223

bad thing. We see no inherent reason why the annual summer trek to the local university is necessarily wasted time if the content of the courses can be made appropriate to principals' needs. Similarly, we think that state principals' associations can be in an excellent position to conduct effective inservice programs for their members, if they organize themselves to do so. (What it may take to accomplish that is strong and determined pressure applied by principals themselves to make their organizations more responsive to their needs.)

At the same time, we would like to see inservice providers increase their repertoires of ways to deliver services to administrators. Nicholson et al. (1977: 6–16) suggest five "general contexts" for inservice education:

1. *Job-embedded.*—Doing the job provides opportunities for activities that can result in professional growth. (We are sure that most principals manage their tenth externally funded project more effecitvely than their first.) Opportunities arise from performing daily tasks, serving on committees, using consultants, and professional reading. Job-embedded inservice is useful because of its unity (with the principal's day-to-day job) and its economy (accomplishing several tasks at once).

2. *Job-related.*—This context includes workshops, exchanges and visits to other schools, the use of training packages, and —perhaps in the near future—mobile computer-assisted instruction.

3. *Credential-oriented.*—Until lately most inservice occurred in the context of satisfying requirements for a credential, especially in traditional university courses taught on campus or near the participant's school through extension services.

4. *Professional-organization related.*—While administrators' associations have probably fallen behind teachers' organizations in providing inservice opportunities to their members, they do offer services such

224

as conferences, workshops, consultation, and professional journals.

5. *Self-directed.*—Principals can puruse a variety of ways of directing their own learning during leisure time, during study leaves or sabbaticals, or by reading, teaching courses in an adjunct professor status at universities, and others.

Within these contexts, a variety of kinds of inservice would be useful to principals; our next four recommendations concern kinds of inservice.

Recommendation #4: Develop a set of materials and strategies on "Administering Change in Schools" that could be used in local or regional seminars for principals in schools with externally funded projects.

We envision here something like looseleaf "yellow pages" or "modules" of training materials, including experiential exercises, role plays, "inbasket" exercises, readings on change, and diagnostic tools. The issues raised in Chapter 3 and the leadership styles, roles, and skills identified in Chapter 4 could serve as a basis for those materials. At a local or regional workshop for principals with externally funded projects, a general format could be presented; principals could then select topics and materials that related most directly to the particular concerns they had.

Recommendation #5: Assist in building a peer support system for principals who administer externally funded projects.

One suggestion consistently made by principals and others was that it would be helpful to visit other schools dealing with projects and concerns similar to their own. We believe that idea could be expanded into an effective staff development program and one in which principals could teach and support each other and themselves with little outside assistance. Funding agencies could assist a few principals in the same geographic area to meet on a regular basis, discuss common concerns, engage in mutual problem-solving, and perhaps create an agenda for inservice training that the funding agency could then help implement.

The two things that would be needed to implement this recommendation are, first, a way of getting information about projects to the persons who need it and, second, a way of encouraging and facilitating meetings and visits. Several funding agencies now do make information like this available. The Colorado State Department of Education in 1977 published a listing and short descriptions of projects concerned with school climate; the department also sponsored a statewide conference dealing with topics related to school climate. We are sure that other states publish similar information. Teacher Corps annually sends to all its projects a wealth of information about other Teacher Corps projects. Through national and state facilitator projects, a national dissemination and information system is slowly being built.

It will probably always be true, however, that printed materials are a fairly inefficient and ineffective way to associate people who can help each other. Doing so will probably require both a push and a pull from funding agencies to bring principals with similar concerns into face-to-face interactions to build a peer support system.

Recommendation #6: Develop a set of job aids for principals to gain understanding and skill in administering special projects.

In our own experience we have found that job aids can provide assistance to a person required to perform a special role. The aids we have in mind include short papers or worksheets such as tips on managing change, pitfalls to avoid at the beginning of a project, checklists of things to do, and materials to guide gathering information. One advantage of job aids is that they can be used when a problem occurs rather than waiting for the next training session. The descriptions of leadership styles, roles, and actions we presented in Chapter 4 could be modified to create checklists, self-scoring instruments on leadership styles, and other guides. The job aids we envision are similar to the Teacher Corps publication *Mapping*

Teacher Corps Projects by Taylor, Sullivan, and Dollar (1978). It is a resource book that highlights issues that must be faced, decisions that must be made, skills that must be used, and people who must be involved. It includes exercises, checklists, data-gathering instruments, and examples from Teacher Corps projects to give assistance and guidance to persons embarking on Teacher Corps projects.

> *Recommendation #7:* Provide information and training to project directors to help them work with principals and assist them with their staff development.

We observed that project directors in the cases—like principals—varied in their abilities to manage their projects and work effectively with principal and staff. It seems to us that a skillful project director could perform a critical function in assisting principals with the management of a change project by providing technical assistance and coaching. (Doing so would probably ease some of the burden of the project director, too.)

For example, in many schools we found that role confusion and conflict were major problems. In other cases, a bit of advice by a project director knowledgeable about change in schools could have averted troubles that were caused by principals who were incautious in their allocation of resources. Sometimes principals were simply unaware of what action would have been useful and the project director might have supplied information to cue the principal to what was needed.

Training for project directors could be similar to the sort of training we envision for principals. It might have more emphasis on ways to clarify role expectations with a superior, ways to get information in a new situation, and skills needed to integrate one's self with the on-going parts of the school.

FUNDING AND SUPPORT

We have not devoted much attention in this book to the questions of providing the funding and support needed for inservice for principals, but we do offer one final recommendation.

227

We think that funding agencies would do well to create incentives to provide inservice training for principals. Several kinds of cooperative arrangements could be found, perhaps by contracting with administrators' associations, private consultants, universities, or other agencies to provide that training.

Recommendation #8: Find ways for various agencies that fund school change projects to cooperate in providing staff development for principals.

In most projects several teachers (or all the teachers in a school) were involved, but normally there was only one administrator, or perhaps a small management team in large schools. That fact makes the logistics of providing training for principals difficult and, if done school-by-school, not very cost-effective. We would like to see agencies such as Teacher Corps, ESEA Title IV-C, Career Education, and others combine resources to provide staff development opportunities for principals within a given state or region.

SUMMARY

We think that the best response to meeting the needs of principals who administer externally funded projects is an eclectic and flexible strategy that focuses on the particular problems of managing those projects and that can be accommodated to a variety of levels of skill and understanding. To create an inservice education program of the kind we envision would require, first, a thorough reconceptulaization of what inservice for administrators can be and should be. One component of that rethinking is new ways of viewing schools; some of the recent literature that describes schools as "organized anarchies" may offer a more realistic and useful conception of educational organizations. Another component is new ideas about how to design and deliver inservice training, consultation, and technical assistance.[7] The traditional view of

---

[7]Our ideas about designing and delivering inservice have been discussed in Arends, Hersh, and Turner (1978) and in a series of "fastback" booklets on inservice education (Wyant and Lovell, 1980).

inservice is too often a linear theory-to-practice model in which the inservice provider describes and prescribes to the practitioner, who in turn delivers services to others. The principal in that model is seen as a passive recipient who is scheduled to "paint by the numbers." David Hunt (1978) offers an alternative view, a "theory-practice-person" conception which directs our attention to building relationships between provider and principal and to the ways in which provider and receiver share responsibility, initiative, and learning.

Another requirement is for additional empirical information about the needs of principals who administer externally funded projects. We did not have available to us, for instance, schools which were marked by the profound problems—financial, racial, and others—that beset urban schools today.[8] We would also like to have confirmation as to the accuracy of our belief that the issues, roles, and skills listed in Chapter 4 are in fact the critical ones for principals and projects.

Finally, we would like to encourage action research by staff development practitioners and inservice providers. We hope that persons trying to design and deliver inservice experiences for principals in schools with externally funded projects will describe their experiences so that a body of literature that is grounded in both theory and experience can be accumulated.

We know of a few programs that embody the kinds of characteristics that we think are important. Nova University requires degree candidates to work in close collaboration with school improvement sites. The Bank Street College (Burnes, et al., 1975) has sponsored a program for elementary principals to help them find the leadership style most suited to them. The Special Education Consultation Project described by Batten and Burello (1975) includes training in organizational development, role clarification, and establishing new norms. The Teacher Center concept could be adapted to the

---

[8]Considerations of providing assistance to urban schools from a viewpoint that closely resembles ours are discussed by Bell (1979) and by Runkel, Schmuck, Arends, and Francisco (1979).

229

needs of principals. Dillion (1974) and Pharis (1966) have proposed highly individualized programs of inservice for principals.

Principals who administer externally funded change projects in their schools comprise a distinct audience for providers of inservice education. They have special needs and special responsibilities that cannot usually be met by traditional methods. We hope that the findings and recommendations in this book can help principals and inservice providers find new ways to meet those needs and that others will take up the challenge of making inservice education a valuable tool that principals can use to meet their responsibilities in managing special projects to create productive and effective situations for teaching and learning.

Interview Protocol for Principals

I PRINCIPAL'S INVOLVEMENT IN PROJECT

I'd like to start by asking you to describe the project briefly.

A. Initiation of the Project

1. The next questions have to do with your first awareness of the project. When did you first hear about it? How did you hear? Who told you or what did you read? What information did you get then?
2. What were your initial reactions to what you heard?
3. Did you do anything yourself to get the project in your school? What did you do? How important do you think that was?
4. What were your thoughts when you first heard the project was going to be in your school?

B. The First 100 Days (Early Implementation)

1. What needs did you identify for your staff at the onset of the project? How did you identify those needs? How much did you involve the staff in planning to meet those needs?
2. Did you see those needs in different terms than did the staff (e.g., budget vs. skill development)?
3. How much of the responsibility for meeting those needs did you turn over to those directly involved in carrying out the project?

C. Full Implementation

1. Did your involvement in project activities change as the project grew and matured? In what ways? Was it more important for you to be involved at one time rather than another? If so, when?
2. Did you detect resistance on the part of your staff at any point? If so, how did you deal with that resistance?

231

3. How have you seen your role in relation to staff members who will be responsible for carrying out the day-to-day activities of the project?
4. What do you feel was the greatest need to be met in order to allow the project to fit and to function in your school?
5. Have you been involved in other projects in your school? Was your involvement with this project the same as with other external projects in your school?
6. Is your role as principal important to the success of a special project? If so, why? Are some things you do with the project more important than others? Please identify those of greatest importance.
7. Do you know of any other principals who have special projects in their schools? From what you've heard, what are the ways in which they helped or hindered the project? What things hindered it?

D. *Summary of Involvement*

1. Consider your total involvement with the project. Can you identify three incidents that show ways in which you positively contributed to the project? Could you describe three incidents that show ways that may have gotten in the way of the project's success?
2. What do you consider to be the greatest benefit from the project?
3. Did your perceptions about the desirability of the project change as the project progressed?
4. Did your perceptions about the staff's enthusiasm for the project change as the project progressed?

II PRINCIPAL'S INSERVICE NEEDS ASSESSMENT

1. Were you expected to do anything with the project you didn't feel sure you could do or wanted to do?
2. What sort of things were you sure you could do?
3. Were inservice activities for administrators a part of the grant? Should they have been?
4. If inservice opportunities were available to you, what kind of training or development experience would you have chosen?
5. What types of inservice activities have you participated in in the past?
6. It is generally believed that the conditions under which administrators work do not provide adequate incentives for them to parcitipate enthusiastically in inservice activities. Is this true? If so, why? What are the major shortcomings of present arrangements?
7. What suggestions do you have for improving the options for administrators to participate in inservice events (e.g., content, training, location, etc.)?
8. Can you think of other ways of offering inservice activities (e.g., other than workshops) for administrators?

9. What are the chief obstacles to reform in this area?
10. What are the chief issues and problems to be solved in developing and implementing better inservice systems for administrators?

III. CONTEXTUAL INFORMATION ABOUT PRINCIPAL

1. Age
2. Ethnic
3. Married/children
4. Years at school, in administration
5. Past professional experience (in/out of school district)
6. Teaching experience
7. Why became administrator
8. Hobbies
9. Leadership style

Now let me summarize what you have said during this interview so I can have you check for accuracy and to assure that your confidentiality has been maintained.

References

Alderfer, Clayton. An empirical test of a new theory of human needs. *Organizational Behavior and Human Performance*, 1969, *4*.

Arends, R. I., R. Hersh, and J. Turner. Inservice education and the six o'clock news. *Theory into Practice*, June 1978, *17*(3).

Arends, R. I., and Jane Phelps. *Establishing Organizational Specialists within School Districts*. Eugene, Ore: Center for Educational Policy and Management, 1973.

Argyris, C., and D. Schon. *Theory into Practice: Increasing Professional Effectiveness*. San Francisco: Jossey-Bass, 1974.

Batten, M. O., and C. C. Burello. *Special Education Simulation and Consultation Project: Special Training Project*. Lansing: Michigan State Department of Education, Michigan University, 1975.

Becker, G., R. Withycombe, F. Doyel, E. Miller, C. Morgan, L. DeLoretta, and B. Aldridge. *Elementary Principals and Their Schools: Beacons of Brilliance and Potholes of Pestilence*. Eugene, Ore.: Center for the Advanced Study of Educational Administration, 1971.

Bell, Warren E. *Impact of Organizational Development Interventions Conducted by an Internal Cadre of Specialists on the Organizational Process in Elementary Schools*. Doctoral Dissertation, Univ. of Oregon, 1977.

———. Obstacles to urban school renewal. *Theory into Practice*, April 1979, *18*(2).

———, Spencer Wyant, and Richard Schmuck. *Diagnosing a School's Readiness for Change: What to Look for When Starting an Innovation*. San Jose: Central California Facilitator Project, 1979.

Berman, Paul, and M. W. McLaughlin. *Federal Programs Supporting Educational Change*, Vol. IV: *The Findings in Review*. Santa Monica, Calif: Rand Corp., 1975.

Blood, R. E. *Factors Affecting the Principalship Yesterday and Today*. Albuquerque: Univ. of New Mexico, Dept of Education, 1978. (Mimeographed.)

Bockman, V. M. *The Principal as Manager of Change*. Speech given before the Colorado Educational Administrators' Conference, 1972.

Burnes, J. C., and associates. *Report of the Program for the Development of the Elementary School Principal as an Educational Leader* (Occasional Paper No. 5). New York: Bank Street College of Education, 1975.

235

Callan, M. F. *Summary of Administrative Inservice Needs Survey*. Eugene, Ore.: Eugene Public Schools, 1979.

Clark, David L. (Ed.). *New Perspectives on Planning in Educational Organizations*. San Francisco: Far West Educational Laboratory, 1980. (Mimeographed.)

Confederation of Oregon School Administrators. *Summary of Needs Survey of COSA Personnel Growth Program*. Salem, Ore.: COSA, 1978. (Mimeographed.)

Denny, Terry. *Story Telling and Educational Understanding* (Occasional Paper Series No. 8). Kalamazoo: Western Michigan Evaluation Center, 1979.

Dillion, E. A., and associates. *Organizing and Expanding the Individualized Continuing Education Program for Administrators in the Local School District: An Occasional Paper*. Denver: Neuva Learning Center, 1974.

Emrick, John A., S. N. Peterson, and R. Agarwala-Rogers. *Evaluation of the National Diffusion Network*. Menlo Park, Calif.: Stanford Research Institute, 1977. (2 vols.)

Firth, Gerald R. Theories of leadership: Where do we stand? *Educational Leadership*, February 1976.

French, Wendell, and C. H. Bell. *Organizational Development*. Englewood Cliffs, N.J.: Prentice-Hall, 1978.

Fullan, Michael, and Alan Pomfret. Research on curriculum and instructional implementation. *Review of Educational Research*, Winter 1977, pp. 335–97.

Gaye, G. Curriculum and the school principal. In C. C. Wersberg (Ed.), *Chicago Principals Reporter*. Chicago: Chicago Principals Association, 1979.

Gmelch, Walt. Beyond stress to effective management. *Oregon School Study Council Bulletin*, May 1977, 20(9).

Goodlad, John, M. F. Klein, and others. *Behind the Classroom Door*. Worthington, Ohio: Charles A. Jones Publishing Co., 1970.

Greenwood, Peter W., Dale Mann, and Milbrey W. McLaughlin. *Federal Programs Supporting Educational Change*, Vol. III: *The Process of Change*. Santa Monica, Calif.: Rand Corp., 1975.

Guba, Egon. *Toward a Methodology of Naturalistic Inquiry in Educational Evaluation*. Los Angeles: Center for the Advanced Study of Educational Evaluation, UCLA, 1978.

Hall, Douglas C., and S. E. Alford. *Evaluation of the National Diffusion Network: Evolution of the Network and Overview of the Research Literature on Diffucion of Educational Innovations*. Menlo Park, Calif.: Stanford Research Institute, 1976.

Halpin, Andrew W. *The Leadership Behavior of School Superintendents*. Chicago: Midwest Administration Center, Univ. of Chicago, 1959.

Harrison, Roger. Materials for "Positive Power and Influence Program." Created by Situation Management Systems, Inc., Boston, 1976.

236

Havelock, Ronald G. *The Change Agent's Guide to Innovation in Education.* Englewood Cliffs, N.J.: Educational Technology Publications, 1973.

Hersey, Paul, and Kenneth H. Blanchard. *Management of Organizational Behavior: Utilizing Human Resources* (3rd Ed.). Englewood Cliffs, N.J.: Prentice-Hall, 1977.

House, Ernest R. *Politics of Educational Innovation.* Berkeley, Calif.: McCutchan, 1974.

Hunt, David E. Inservice training as persons-in-relation. *Theory into Practice,* June 1978, *17*(3), 239–44.

Jongewood, Dorothy. *Everybody Wins: Transactional Analysis Applied to Organizations.* Reading, Mass.: Addison Wesley, 1974.

Joyce, Bruce R., Kenneth Howey, and Sam J. Yarger. *Inservice Teacher Education.* Vols. 1–5. Palo Alto, Calif.: Stanford Center for Research and Development in Teaching, 1976.

Latta, F. *A Synopsis of the California Teacher Corps Network Survey: The Inservice Needs of Teacher Corps Building Principals.* San Diego: San Diego State Univ., Dept. of Educational Administration, 1978.

Likert, Rensis. *The Human Organization.* New York: McGraw-Hill, 1967.

Lipham, J. M. The administrator's role in education linkage. In N. Nash and J. Culbertson, *Linking Processes in Educational Improvement.* Columbus, Ohio: Univ. Council for Educational Administration, 1977.

Lovell, Katherine. *Introduction to Responsive Inservice Education* (Title One in Responsive Inservice Education Series). Eugene, Ore.: Teacher Corps Project, Univ. of Oregon, 1980.

McCleary, Lloyd E., and Scott D. Thomson. *The Senior High School Principalship.* Vol. III: *The Summary Report.* Reston, Va.: National Assn. of Secondary School Principals, 1979.

McClelland, D. C. Methods of measuring human motivation. In J. W. Atkinson (Ed.), *Motives in Fantasy, Action and Society.* New York: Van Nostrand, 1958.

Maguire, Louis M., Sanford Temkin, and C. Peter Cummings. *An Annotated Bibliography on Administering for Change.* Philadelphia: Research for Better Schools, Inc., 1971.

Maier, Norman R. F. *Problem-Solving and Creativity in Individuals and Groups.* Belmont, Calif.: Brooks/Cole Publishing Co., 1970.

Mann, Dale. *Design Specifications for a User-Proven, Federally Supported System of School Improvement.* New York: Columbia Univ., 1976. (Mimeographed.)

_____.Making change happen. *Teachers College Record,* February 1976.

Maslow, A. *Motivation and Personality.* New York: Harper and Row, 1954.

Miles, M. B. *Innovation in Education.* New York: Columbia University Teachers College, 1964.

237

_____. *Tehnographic Methods and Their Problems.* New York: Center for Policy Research, Nov. 24, 1978(a). (Mimeographed.)

_____. *Executive Summary, Project on Social Architecture in Education.* New York: Center for Policy Research, 1978(b). (Mimeographed.)

Nicholson, Alexander M., and Bruce R. Joyce, with D. W. Parker and F. T. Waterman. *The Literature on Inservice Teacher Education: An Analytic Review.* Palo Alto, Calif.: Stanford Center for Research and Development in Teaching, 1977.

Paul, D. A. Change processes at the elementary, secondary, and postsecondary levels in education. In N. Nash and J. Culbertson (Eds.), *Linking Processes in Educational Improvement.* Columbus, Ohio: Univ. Council for Educational Administration, 1977.

Pharis, W. L. *Inservice Education of Elementary School Principals.* Washington, D.C.: National Educational Association, 1966.

Reinhard, Diane, Richard Arends, William Kutz, and Spencer Wyant. *A Study of the Principal's Role in Externally-Funded Change Projects and the Implications for Inservice Training.* Vol. I: *Technical Report.* Vol. II: *Case Studies* (edited by Katherine Lovell). Eugene, Ore: Teacher Corps Project, Univ. of Oregon, 1979. (Mimeographed.)

Runkel, Philip J., and Ann Burr. *Bibliography on Organizational Change in Schools.* Eugene, Ore: Center for Educational Policy and Management, 1977.

Runkel, P. J., R. A. Schmuck, J. Arends, and R. P. Francisco. *Transforming the School's Capacity for Problem Solving.* Eugene, Ore.: Center for Educational Policy and Management, 1979.

Runkel, P. J., S. H. Wyant, W. E. Bell, and M. Runkel. *Organizational Renewal in a School District.* Eugene, Ore.: Center for Educational Policy and Management, 1980.

Sarason, Seymour B. *The Culture of the School and the Problem of Change.* Boston: Allyn and Bacon, 1971.

Schmuck, Richard A., Donald Murray, Mary Ann Smith, Mitchell Schwartz, and Margaret Runkel. *Consultation for Innovative Schools: OD for Multiunit Structure.* Eugene, Ore.: Center for Educational Policy and Management, 1975.

Schmuck, R. A., and J. E. Nelson. The principal as convener of organizational change. *Research Reports in Educational Administration* (Boulder, Colo.), 1970, 2(2).

Schmuck, R. A., P. Runkel, and J. Arends. *The Second Handbook of Organization Development in Schools.* Palo Alto, Calif.: Mayfield Publishing Co., 1977.

Sieber, S. E., K. S. Louis, and L. Metzhar. *The Use of Educational Knowledge: Evaluation of the Pilot State Dissemination Programs.* New York: Columbia Univ., Bureau of Applied Social Research, 1972. (2 vols.)

Silberman, Charles E. *Crisis in the Classroom: The Remaking of American Education*. New York: Vintage Books, 1970.

Simons, David L. *Durability of Organizational Training for a School Faculty*. Doctoral dissertation, Univ. of Oregon, 1974.

Smith, Mary Ann. *A Comparison of Two Elementary Schools Involved in a Major Organizational Change: Or You Win a Few, You Lose a Few*. Doctoral dissertation, Univ. of Oregon, 1972.

Stake, Robert E. *The Logic of the Case Study*. Unpublished paper, CIRCE, Univ. of Ill., March 1976.

_____. *Field Work Guidelines*. Unpublished paper, CIRCE, Univ. of Ill., 1977.

_____. *Sweet Waters*. Paper prepared for the American Educational Research Association Series, 1979.

_____, and Jack A. Easley. *Case Studies in Science Education*. Vol. II: *Design, Overview and General Findings*. Urbana: Center for Instructional Research and Curriculum Evaluation, Univ. of Ill., January 1978.

Starling, William. *An Unsuccessful Attempt to Implement an Educational Innovation: A Case Study*. Doctoral dissertation, Univ. of Oregon, 1973.

Swaab, Alexander M. Organizational change and the principal. *Journal of Educational Technology*, 1972, *12*(10).

Tannenbaum, Robert, and Warren H. Schmidt. How to choose a leadership pattern. *Harvard Business Review*, May-June 1973, *51*(3).

Taylor, Beverley L., Ellen W. Sullivan, and Bruce Dollar. *Mapping Teacher Corps Projects*. New York: Center for Policy Research, 1978.

Tomkins, E., and J. L. Trump. *The Secondary School Principalship and the Challenge of Change*. 1969. (Mimeographed.) ERIC Number: ED 030 185.

Townsend, Robert. *Up the Organization*. New York: Knopf, 1970.

Wellman, Joan. *Unsystematic Features of Organizations: Implications for Management Training*. Eugene: Univ. of Oreg, 1980. (Mimeographed.)

Wolcott, Harry. *The Man in the Principal's Office: An Ethnography*. New York: Holt, Rinehart and Winston, 1973.

_____. *Teachers versus Technocrats*. Eugene, Ore.: Center for Educational Policy and Management, 1977.

Wolf, Robert L., and Barbara L. Tymitz. *A Preliminary Guide for Conducting Natural Inquiry in Studying Museum Environments*. Indiana Univ., Indiana Center for Evaluation, 1978.

Wyant, Spencer H., and Katherine Lovell (Eds.). *Series on Responsive Inservice Education*. Eugene: Univ. of Oregon, Teacher Corps Project, 1980.